warmest regards!

[signature]
22 Oct '13

THE 9TH INFANTRY DIVISION IN VIETNAM

American Warriors

Throughout the nation's history, numerous men and women of all ranks and branches of the United States military have served their country with honor and distinction. During times of war and peace, there are individuals whose exemplary achievements embody the highest standards of the U.S. armed forces. The aim of the American Warriors series is to examine the unique historical contributions of these individuals, whose legacies serve as enduring examples for soldiers and citizens alike. The series will promote a deeper and more comprehensive understanding of the U.S. armed forces.

SERIES EDITOR: Roger Cirillo

An AUSA Book

THE 9TH INFANTRY DIVISION IN VIETNAM

Unparalleled and Unequaled

Major General Ira A. Hunt Jr.,
USA (Ret.)

THE UNIVERSITY PRESS OF KENTUCKY

Copyright © 2010 by The University Press of Kentucky

Scholarly publisher for the Commonwealth,
serving Bellarmine University, Berea College, Centre
College of Kentucky, Eastern Kentucky University,
The Filson Historical Society, Georgetown College,
Kentucky Historical Society, Kentucky State University,
Morehead State University, Murray State University,
Northern Kentucky University, Transylvania University,
University of Kentucky, University of Louisville,
and Western Kentucky University.
All rights reserved.

Editorial and Sales Offices: The University Press of Kentucky
663 South Limestone Street, Lexington, Kentucky 40508-4008
www.kentuckypress.com

14 13 12 11 10   5 4 3 2 1

Library of Congress Cataloging-in-Publication Data

Hunt, Ira Augustus, 1924–
  The 9th Infantry Division in Vietnam : unparalleled and unequaled / Ira A. Hunt Jr.
    p.   cm. — (American warriors)
  Includes bibliographical references and index.
  ISBN 978-0-8131-2647-0 (hardcover : alk. paper) —
  ISBN 978-0-8131-2648-7 (ebook)
  1. Vietnam War, 1961–1975—Regimental histories—United States.
2. United States. Army. Infantry Division, 9th. 3. Vietnam War,
1961–1975—Campaigns. I. Title. II. Title: Ninth Infantry Division in Vietnam.
  DS558.4.H85 2010
  959.704'342—dc22
                           2010032803

This book is printed on acid-free recycled paper meeting
the requirements of the American National Standard
for Permanence in Paper for Printed Library Materials.

Manufactured in the United States of America.

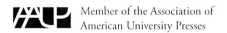

Member of the Association of
American University Presses

To the valiant soldiers of the 9th Infantry Division in Vietnam

Contents

List of Maps and Figures   viii
List of Tables   x
Abbreviations and Special Terms   xi

Introduction   1
  1. Securing the Mekong Delta   4
  2. The General Offensive and General Uprising   12
  3. Enhancing Combat Capabilities   22
  4. Pacification: The Endgame   79
  5. Third Phase of the VC/NVA General Offensive   99
  6. Fourth Phase of the VC/NVA General Offensive   111
  7. The Take-off   116
  8. Post–Dong Xuan Operations   137
  9. Pacification Results   141
  10. A Total Division Effort   147
  11. The Division Rotates Home   150

Appendix A. 9th Infantry Division and Assigned and Attached Units, 1969   157
Appendix B. 9th Infantry Division Task Organization, January–April 1969   159
Appendix C. The Story of a Booby-Trap Casualty   160
Appendix D. Prisoner Phan Xuan Quy: Biographical Information and Thanh Phu Battle Account   164
Appendix E. Reflection of a Prisoner   175
Notes   177
Index   180

Maps and Figures

Maps

1. 9th Infantry Division tactical area of responsibility, 31 August 1968   33
2. Counter operations of 520th Battalion at Thuan My village, 12 August 1968   104
3. Sketch maps, Battle of Thanh Phu, 11–12 March 1969   168

Figures

1. Rice paddy with troops crossing a stream   9
2. Tango boats on the Mekong   10
3. Battle of Saigon   20
4. Dong Tam base camp   26
5. Stream-crossing in Long An Province   31
6. A Tiger Scout   34
7. Relocating artillery   37
8. Critical trooper—helicopter mechanic   44
9. Slicks at a landing zone   59
10. A pick-up zone   62
11. Sgt. Adelbert Waldron takes aim   69
12. Soldier on a rice-paddy dike   73
13. Hamlet Evaluation System model hierarchy   83
14. Viet Cong propaganda leaflet   88
15. MEDCAP   89
16. ARVN soldiers   94
17. Captured VC weapons   98

18. Taking ten   109
19. Constant muck and water   115
20. Combat casualty   140
21. Afternoon stroll   145
22. Church service   149

Tables

1. Aircraft combat effectiveness   40
2. Reliability of intelligence resources   51
3. Bushmaster operations   63
4. Checkerboard operations   64
5. Ambushes   66
6. Sniper kills   68
7. Night Search operations   75
8. Hamlet control situation   84
9. Hamlet Evaluation Ratings, Kien Hoa   85
10. Operational effectiveness, recommended goals   93
11. Quarterly results of military operations, 1967–1969   97
12. Communist battalions involved in general offensives   100
13. Quarterly operational report, 1967–1968   106
14. Enemy eliminated, day and night   108
15. Box score, Battle of Thanh Phu   128
16. Quarterly operational report, January, February, March 1969   135
17. Major unit contacts, April and May 1969   138
18. Operations, 27 March–26 April 1969   139
19. Viet Cong population control   142
20. Statistical results, February 1967–July 1969   155

Abbreviations and Special Terms

AO	Area of Operations
ARVN	Army of the Republic of Vietnam
Bushmaster	A company or platoon-sized unit is inserted into an area and establishes a base of operations to interdict enemy LOCs from carefully selected ambush sites
Checkerboard	A night operation in which several squad or platoon-sized patrols constantly maneuver from one area or terrain feature to another, seeking to contact the enemy
Chieu Hoi	A GVN established program to entice Communists to rally to the government side
COMUSMACV	Commander, U.S. Military Assistance Command, Vietnam
COSVN	Central Office South Vietnam; this is the Communist headquarters controlling all operations in southern South Vietnam
Corps tactical zone	The GVN established four military regions, each headed by a corps commander, and military operations within the MR were in the corps tactical zone
DMZ	The Demarcation Zone, which separated South Vietnam from North Vietnam
G-2	The division-level intelligence officer
G-3	The division-level operations officer
GVN	The Government of South Vietnam
HES	Hamlet Evaluation Survey

Hoi Chanh	A Communist who has defected to the GVN
HUMINT	Intelligence obtained through human resources
ICAP	A medical civic action program generally conducted in contested hamlets whose objective was to gather intelligence
Jitterbug	A tactic employing assault helicopters to make multiple insertions and extractions of troops on selected targets until contact is established
JGS	South Vietnamese Joint General Staff
LOC	Line of communications
LZ	Landing zone
KHA	U.S. soldiers killed by hostile action
KIA	Enemy killed in action
MACV	Military Assistance Command, Vietnam
MEDCAP	A humanitarian operation conducted by medical personnel to treat South Vietnamese villagers
MR	Military region
MRF	Mobile riverine force
NCO	Noncommissioned officer
NITECAP	An ICAP that stayed overnight in a contested area to bring security to the hamlet/village for psychological purposes
Night Search	A night airborne operation utilizing a spotter aircraft carrying riflemen with night vision devices and a light-fire team to interdict enemy infiltration routes
Night Raid	A daring night operation where combat troops are inserted by helicopter into an area to kill or capture Communist troops
NVA	North Vietnamese Army
OPCON	Operational control
Paddy strength	The number of infantrymen in the field on combat operations
PF	South Vietnamese popular forces
PSDF	People Self Defense Force
PZ	Pick-up zone

RF	South Vietnamese regional forces
RVNAF	Republic of Vietnam Armed Forces
Search and pile-on	The positioning of friendly units around an engaged enemy force so as to cut off all escape routes thereby enabling massive friendly artillery, Air Force, and ground firepower to destroy the enemy
Spooky	A U.S. or South Vietnamese Air Force C-47 flareship equipped with mini-guns and capable of providing one and a half hours of battlefield illumination
TAOI	Tactical area of interest
TAOR	Tactical area of responsibility
Tiger Scout	Those Hoi Chanhs who completed the Chieu Hoi (Open Arms) Program and were hired by the 9th Division to work with our combat infantry units
VC	Viet Cong
VCI	Viet Cong Infrastructure personnel
WHA	Wounded in Hostile Action

Introduction

In the mid-1960s, the security of the Delta, the densely populated rich rice bowl of agrarian South Vietnam, was poor and getting worse. Viet Cong (VC) insurgents were severely disrupting the commerce and welfare of this vital region. The 9th Infantry Division, the only U.S. Army division activated and trained in the United States for active duty in South Vietnam, was specifically designated to operate from a base deep within the Communist-controlled Delta with the mission to improve the security of the area so that the Government of South Vietnam's (GVN) pacification program could be successful. Upon its arrival in Vietnam in February 1967, the division from day one focused on finding and eliminating the oppressive enemy and on assisting the GVN in its pacification efforts.

This book covers the two and a half years of the 9th Division's operations in South Vietnam, focusing primarily on the period from May 1968 until July 1969, when, its mission successfully completed, the division rotated back to the States. That was generally the period of my assignment as division chief of staff, and it includes several personal accounts. This is the story of how the 9th Infantry Division—with astute management and by employing all-source intelligence coupled with aggressive, innovative night and day tactical operations—was able to peak in combat effectiveness in 1969. The division's tactic of unrelenting pressure provides a blueprint for defeating enemy forces fighting a guerrilla war in a rural environment.

This constant pressure concept required continuous operations throughout our area, both night and day. For example, every night gutsy squads of infantrymen established scores of ambushes deep within VC territory and every day our brave soldiers conducted multiple helicopter assaults to find and bring the enemy to battle:

"If you take the most rotten and inaccessible place you can find in this country and put infantrymen there, you'll almost always find VC," said 1st Lieutenant Craig Bennett, platoon leader with the 1st Brigade. "They know Americans hate to go there with the leeches and booby traps, so they'll hide in stinking water up to their necks until we walk right up and pull them out. But that's the only way you can fight a war in the Delta."

Excerpts, like this quotation from a 9th Division submission for Recommendation for Award of the Presidential Unit Citation, have been used to present actual combat experiences of the valiant soldiers of the division, including reports of several major battles.[1] Maj. Jack O. Bradshaw, an outstanding staff officer, prepared that submission under my direction. These quoted excerpts are indented in the text for easy identification.

The division at all times concentrated on obtaining results in all activities, including logistics, administration, tactics, and pacification. Each activity (input) had a result (output). The results were normally measurable and quantifiable; the ratios of outputs to inputs were considered a gross measure of efficiency that normalized our statistics, enabling us to deduce rough standards of effectiveness. This analytical approach to operations was also tempered by military judgment.

Our concentration on getting results enabled combat capabilities to be continuously improved by optimizing the availability of the Infantry soldier, increasing helicopter availability, integrating intelligence, and improving tactics and techniques.[2]

In a one-month period starting in late March 1969, the division had 3,572 operations, over a hundred per day, 60 percent of which were conducted at night, resulting in 1,120 contacts eliminating over three thousand enemy (see table 18, on page 139). The pace and intensity of operations under the constant pressure concept are difficult to comprehend.

The division's accomplishments led the normally understated Gen. Creighton Abrams to say, at Dong Tam, on 2 April 1969, "The performance of this division has been magnificent and I would say in the last three months it's an unparalleled and unequaled performance."

However, several individuals have expressed doubts that the 9th Division could have had such a high level of combat success. My motivation for writing this compendium of the operations of the 9th Division has thus been twofold. I want, first, to enlighten those who disparage the division's combat record in eliminating the enemy and pacifying the Mekong Delta region without comprehending the pace and intensity of its highly innovative combat operations and, second, to provide examples of the bravery and dedication of all the 9th Division soldiers who operated night and day in the inundated and inhospitable Delta—which was infested everywhere with mines and booby traps—to ferret out and destroy a highly elusive VC and NVA enemy.

With respect to pacification, the control of the Delta countryside was paramount to the GVN in the 1967–1969 period of guerrilla warfare, since it would take away from the Communists their major source of sustenance and manpower and deny them the bases from which to attack urban areas. Our pacification efforts were integrated as much as possible with combat operations. We extensively utilized the MACV Hamlet Evaluation Survey to plan and monitor results. Since the endgame was GVN pacification, we coordinated continuously with all echelons of the GVN, including local, district, and provincial personnel. We conducted joint operations with ARVN troops, trained ARVN in ground and airborne operations, worked with the National Police Force, and maintained continuous liaison with the RVNAF JGS.

The grateful GVN on two occasions awarded the 9th Division the Vietnamese Cross of Gallantry for its highly effective counterinsurgency operations, which brought security and pacification to the Delta area. The GVN also granted its Civic Action Medal to the division for its pacification results, the first time that recognition had ever been given to a military unit. Even the North Vietnamese acknowledge the successful pacification outcome, stating during the 1967–1969 period, "The RVNAF was very successful in the pacification of the Mekong Delta" (see chapter 11, "Pacification Results").

The soldiers of the 9th Infantry Division in Vietnam in this two-and-a-half-year period distinguished themselves by their outstanding performance of duty and their extraordinary heroism in action against enemy forces. They successfully overcame the extremely hazardous and difficult Delta terrain and inflicted defeat after defeat upon an elusive enemy. The mission of the division when it was introduced into the Delta was to deny the Communists access to the resources of the region and to improve security so that the political and social aspects of the GVN's pacification program could occur. That mission was accomplished.

Chapter 1

Securing the Mekong Delta

The Mekong Delta was the most populated and richest agrarian area of South Vietnam, and consequently it was the primary target of Communist aggression. Viet Cong activities in the Delta were appreciably reducing the cultivation of the important rice crop and were isolating the Delta from Saigon. It became obvious that increased military actions were necessary to deny the Communists access to the Delta's resources. It was the opinion of Gen. William Childs Westmoreland that any substantial improvement in security required the introduction of U.S. forces, and the 9th Infantry Division was activated in the States to assist in securing the delta so that the Government of South Vietnam's (GVN) pacification program could become successful.

The Communists' Primary Target

The avowed goal of the North Vietnamese Communist insurgency in South Vietnam was to control the maximum amount of land and numbers of people for two reasons: first, for the political cachet this control brought to their claims of sovereignty, and second, for the support it brought to their military operations. South Vietnam was an agrarian society with the large majority of the population living in rural areas, dependent upon agricultural production to eke out a meager living. Many of the peasants were tenant farmers, illiterate and medically ill-cared-for; they were sometimes plagued by corrupt officials and often taken advantage of by greedy landlords. Unquestionably, the peasants of the rural area were the least privileged of Vietnamese society, and for that reason, they were the most susceptible to Communist indoctrination, which preached class warfare. Consequently, the countryside was the primary target of the Communist insurgency. Conversely, the pacification of the rural area was the major goal of the GVN, which desired to bring security and economic and political stability to the area.

In the early 1960s, the GVN pacification program was doing quite well, with about two-thirds of the rural population settled in strategic hamlets, effectively separating the population from the Communists. However, after the political unrest in 1963, particularly the coup d'état that resulted in the discontinuance of the Strategic Hamlet Program, the Communists took control of the countryside. Even though rural area pacification was of vital importance to the GVN, they focused their pacification efforts in the mid-1960s primarily on population centers and provincial and district capitols—the "oil blob strategy" whereby the GVN intended to expand its control outward from these nuclei, ultimately reclaiming all of the countryside. This was prudent; at the time the GVN did not have the organization to effect control of the thousands of villages and hamlets. The strategy was ultimately successful, because, by 1973, the GVN controlled 92 percent of the population and most of the territory.

In the mid-1960s, the Communists were well organized, with a multitiered structure to take and maintain control of the rural villages and hamlets. At the apex of their structure were the well-trained and experienced main force units, supported in combat operations by local force units, which generally operated in the vicinity of their homes, where they knew the terrain and people. The main and local force units provided the cover for the guerrilla forces, which were also localized and whose responsibility it was to support the combat units by transporting supplies, constructing defenses, and providing intelligence as well as conducting harassment and sabotage actions. The guerrillas were a primary source of manpower for Communist combat units. Finally, a vital cog in the Communist hierarchy was the Infrastructure, which at the grass-roots level collected taxes, provided intelligence, and assisted in recruiting. All elements were supported by a well-honed propaganda organization whose activities took advantage of the people's discontent.

Comparatively, the GVN had not yet effected the organization necessary to conduct a successful pacification program. The Army was expanding and refitting with U.S. support. At the local level, there were civil guards and the self defense corps, but they were poorly equipped and led. As stated, the GVN units had withdrawn into population enclaves, so the Communists pretty much had the run of the countryside. Their control of the abundant resources and manpower of the rural areas provided the Communists the capability to attack the GVN urban strongholds, and the military situation was deteriorating. It was at this point, in 1965, that the United States sent in troops to attempt to stabilize the situation.

If the main conflict raging in South Vietnam was a tug-of-war for the allegiance of the peasant population, then the key battlefield was the Mekong Delta, a densely inhabited alluvial plain extending south and west of Saigon. It contained almost half of South Vietnam's population, and its fertile soil was the source of rice production, the main crop that fed the nation. This predominantly rural area was the primary target of the Communist insurgency, for it was its main source of manpower and sustenance.

The Requirement for Improved Security in the Mekong Delta

In 1965 in the Mekong Delta, the Government of South Vietnam (GVN) was losing the periodic "rice war," which was fought seasonally to control the rice harvest. Viet Cong activities in the Delta had appreciably reduced cultivation, and the VC were forcibly appropriating a large amount of the crop; what they couldn't take they bought. Thus, the quantity of rice available to the GVN to feed its population was at an all-time low, well below the consumption level, thereby requiring the importation of rice into this normally rice-sufficient economy. The Viet Cong activities were also highly disruptive in many other matters, creating severe hardships for the population. It was obvious to all concerned that military actions had to be taken to deny the Communists access to the Delta's resources and improve security so that the political and social aspects of the GVN's pacification programs could take root.

The Mekong Delta is a unique area for conducting military operations, and the terrain and vegetation of the Delta created important limitations on the use of combat power. The land surface is extremely low and flat, at an average of about two meters above sea level. Surface drainage is poor, because of the lack of gradients necessary to create decent run-off conditions. Therefore, the region is usually inundated with brackish or stagnant water. Several large rivers have, over time, deposited the rich alluvial soil forming the Delta, and they, along with a series of major canals constructed by the French to reclaim land for rice farming, provide the drainage network, which in turn is connected by a great number of smaller canals and streams. Thus, the area is a virtual maze of streams and canals, making cross-country foot movement slow and arduous. Rice paddies are everywhere, making foot travel even more difficult when they are flooded. The rice paddy dikes, generally several feet high and about two feet wide, are the most common relief features. Throughout the area, there are small elevations of land, and these are generally where the hamlets are located. Almost all the waterways are lined with a dense growth of vegetation, which provides excellent concealment. Additionally, there are palm groves scattered throughout the area. The vegetative growth provides fair cover from aerial observation. However, the wide open nature of the rice paddies provides no cover. Thus, the open terrain is ideally suitable for helicopter operations, presenting excellent choices for landing zones. On the other hand, once troops have landed, they have to advance with difficulty through the muck of the rice paddies, exposed to observation and oftentimes to enemy fire.

The temperature in the Delta is relatively constant throughout the year, with the average monthly lows and highs ranging between 75° and 90° F. There are two definite monsoonal seasons, the wet and the dry. The wet season, from mid-May through October, has an average rainfall of about eight inches per month, making military operations in the low-lying terrain extremely difficult. Thunderstorms, prevalent in the wet season, can adversely affect helicopter operations. The dry season, from November to mid-May, has an average monthly rainfall of only about one-half inch.

The Delta is rather inhospitable. The whole area contains malaria-bearing mosquitoes. The canals and rice paddies have microorganisms and fungi that can cause serious skin problems, particularly of the feet. Snakes and leeches make troops uncomfortable, and wasps are a constant problem.

The major waterways, canals, and streams that crisscross the area facilitate the rapid movement of enemy troops and supplies by sampan, the vehicle of choice for the Communists. The region has diurnal tides ranging from six to ten feet, so there are normally four tidal changes per day, a matter of importance when operating on the rivers.

In late 1965, notwithstanding the obvious difficulties unacclimated troops would have operating in the hostile Delta environment, it was the opinion of General Westmoreland, the COMUSMACV, that any substantial improvement in Delta security required the introduction of U.S. forces. Until then, the advisors to the RVNAF units were the only U.S. presence in the Delta. The Communists, trumpeting to the world that the conflict in Vietnam was an indigenous insurrection, had carefully refrained from introducing NVA units or personnel into the region; however, they continuously supplied the Viet Cong with weapons and supplies. There were many Americans, particularly in the U.S. embassy, who were against the involvement of U.S. ground troops because of the possibility of collateral damage in the densely populated area. However, MACV, with the approval of the GVN, requested an additional U.S. infantry division to be employed in the Delta. The request was approved by the Pentagon.

Activation of the 9th Infantry Division

To fulfill General Westmoreland's request for a U.S. division, the 9th Infantry Division, under the command of Maj. Gen. George S. Eckhardt, was activated at Fort Riley, Kansas, on 1 February 1966 and after its training was scheduled to operate in the Mekong Delta. At the same time, studies were ongoing in Vietnam to determine the optimal location for basing the Division in the Delta. The MACV staff, noting that the French earlier had been successful in riverine operations in the Delta, which had over three thousand miles of navigable rivers and canals, formulated a concept for a brigade-sized riverine force. The Viet Cong had established several major base areas inaccessible by road, where they operated with impunity, and it was considered that a riverine assault force would be able to invade those sanctuaries. Therefore, in establishing criteria for the location of a divisional base camp in the Delta, one criterion was ready access to the Delta waterways. Other criteria were that the location had to be deep within Viet Cong territory and that the land required, about six hundred acres, should not displace people or cultivated areas. The displacement criterion could

Fig. 1. Rice paddy with troops crossing a stream

not be met, and it was decided to construct an area by hydraulically pumping sand from the Mekong River. A site was chosen five miles from the important river port of My Tho, and huge hydraulic dredges pumped 17 million cubic yards of sand to elevate the area some eight feet. Actual construction of the 12,500-man cantonment began in January 1967. Westmoreland personally chose the name of the base camp, "Dong Tam," which means "united hands and minds," an excellent choice considering that the purpose of the introduction of U.S. ground forces into the Delta was to enhance the ongoing Pacification Program by bringing security to the area.[1]

Concurrent with the activation of the 9th Division, planning progressed with the U.S. Navy in the development of a riverine force that would employ two infantry battalions afloat, enabling the force to be highly mobile, capable of sustained operations over a wide area. This unique Brigade was to be based aboard Navy ships and Navy armored troop carriers (Tango boats) would transport infantrymen to assault areas.

The main body of the 9th Division closed in Vietnam on 1 Febru-

Fig. 2. Tango boats on the Mekong

ary 1967, one year to the day after its activation. Initially, the division was given a large tactical area of interest that included all or parts of eight Vietnamese provinces. Limited combat operations commenced almost immediately. In March, the 3rd Brigade was sent to operate in the Delta's Long An Province in the III Corps Tactical Zone (CTZ). The 2nd Brigade was stationed at Dong Tam to guard the construction of the divisional base camp and operated in the Delta's Dinh Tuong and Kien Hoa Provinces in the IV Corps Tactical Zone until it was established as the mobile riverine force (MRF) in June 1967. Col. William B. Fulton, the 2nd Brigade commander, and his staff did a truly outstanding job in planning, coordinating, and training his troops within a compressed time period to prepare them for joint riverine operations with the U.S. Navy, enabling the MRF to deploy quickly for combat operations in the Delta.[2] Upon deployment aboard naval vessels, the 2nd Brigade was replaced by the 1st Brigade. The Division Headquarters, several battalions of the 1st Brigade, and the bulk of the divisional support troops were located at Camp Martin Cox, known as Bearcat, a base camp located fifteen miles east of Saigon.

By late 1967, the 3rd Brigade was still operating in Long An Province, the 1st Brigade operated in Dinh Tuong Province, and its battalions based at Bearcat shared responsibility for the western portion of Long Khanh Province with the Royal Thai Army Regiment (the Queen's Cobra), which was under the 9th Division's operational control. The 2nd Brigade, the MRF, ranged far and wide, utilizing the waterways to attack Viet Cong base areas in the upper Delta. The MRF was most successful in its early operations because the enemy fortifications which were normally dug in along the many canals and rivers were sited to defend against overland approaches and helicopter assaults and were not oriented to defend against attacks by troops assaulting from naval ATCs. However, after about six months, the Viet Cong in the upper Delta had pretty much learned to cope with the Riverine Force and, in fact, were beginning to establish ambushes along the waterways. This split disposition of the division and operational areas remained about the same until the division headquarters moved from Bearcat to Dong Tam in late June 1968.

Chapter 2

The General Offensive and General Uprising

In 1967, the Communists assumed that the RVNAF and Allied Forces were weak and could be defeated so they abandoned their limited offensive tactics and adopted the concept of large battles, generally conducted by main force units. Thus, the Communists changed their tactics from company- and platoon-sized or smaller operations to battles conducted with multibattalion attacks. For example, on 10 December 1967, at An Naut Tan, the 2/60 Infantry was attacked by the 2nd Independent Battalion supported by the 506th Battalion and the 5th Nha Be Battalion. Hanoi subsequently decided to implement the "General Offensive and General Uprising" plan of the war in 1967–1969. The offensive was to be conducted throughout South Vietnam in several phases by Viet Cong main force units attacking cities and U.S. and RVNAF military units and installations. The Communists believed that with tactical victories, the people of South Vietnam would rally behind the Communist cause, thus leading to the overthrow of the government, the so-called General Uprising.

First Phase of the VC/NVA General Offensive, Tet

The first phase of the Communist General Offensive was launched on 30 January 1968, when the enemy breached its self-declared Tet holidays cease-fire to launch countrywide, all-out attacks against provincial and district capitols and U.S. and GVN military installations. A significant change in these attacks by the Communists was the use of daylight assaults on their targets to include major cities. Using these tactics, they sustained heavy losses; however, they entrenched themselves in many built-up areas, terrorizing the populace and inflicting widespread damage to property. Obviously, the Viet Cong activities were designed to disrupt the economy, thus discrediting the GVN and convincing the population of VC control. In that respect, a main Communist goal was disruption of the major lines of communication, particularly in the rice-rich Delta regions, primarily Route 4, the People's Road.

In the III Corps area, the main attacks were conducted against Saigon (including Tan Son Nhut Air Base), Bien Hoa (including the air base), Long Binh (including II Field Force Headquarters), Tan An, and Xuan Loc. In the IV Corps area, the major attacks were on the cities of My Tho, Ben Tre, Can Tho, and Vinh Long. The 9th Infantry Division, as the major U.S. combat unit south of Saigon, aggressively countered these attacks over several weeks. It deployed units rapidly with minimum advance warning and demonstrated great flexibility by operating effectively in many different areas.[1]

The 4/39 Infantry Battalion and the 2/47 Mechanized Infantry Battalion initially provided security for the major U.S. military installations at Long Binh and Bien Hoa. However, on 2 February, the 4/39 Infantry air-mobilized to Nha Be to relieve the enemy pressure on Saigon from VC forces that withdrew to the outer edges of Saigon after the initial Tet attack. The 2/39 Infantry Battalion operating in Long An was OPCON to the 3rd Brigade and, with the 2/60 Infantry Battalion and the 3/39 Infantry Battalion, airmobiled to Ben Tre, the capital of Kien Hoa, where they successfully defended the city and swept it clean of the VC. Ultimately, the brigade was given the mission of opening the vital Highway 4 from My Tho to Cai Lay, which it did by extensive day-and-night ambushes and aggressive patrolling.

On 31 January, the MRF was moved from its pre-Tet blocking position in western Dinh Tuong Province to My Tho in response to a multibattalion VC assault on that capital city. The MRF was made OPCON to the senior advisor IV Corp, who, incidentally, was Major General George S. Eckhardt, the initial commanding general of the newly activated 9th Division. In the summer of 1967, Maj. Gen. George G. O'Connor, formerly the assistant division commander, followed Eckhardt in command of the division. On 1 February, two battalions landed and attacked north from the My Tho River into the city, where they engaged the 261, 263, and 265 VC Battalions, which were occupying the city. After clearing My Tho, with the support of the 7th ARVN Division, two battalions of the 2nd Brigade were transported by helicopter and sent to assist the RVNAF in clearing Vinh Long. Finally, the 2nd Brigade moved to Can Tho to relieve VC pressure on that capital. In three weeks of continuous fighting, the division decisively defeated the major Communist attacks in the Mekong Delta. No question about it, the courageous men of the 2nd Brigade helped to save the Delta.

The 3rd Brigade missions were to reduce the VC and NVA threats to the Capitol Military District and to maintain pressure on the enemy in Long An Province, disrupting his infiltration routes. The 5/60 Infantry Battalion OPCON to the 1st Brigade operated in the Capitol Military District in the vicinity of the Phu Tho Race Track. As mentioned, the brigade cleared Ben Tre. On 10 February, Tan An came under a severe attack, and the enemy was repulsed with heavy losses.

During the first phase of the Communist General Offensive and General Uprising, the division provided security to vital installations and aggressively rooted out the VC from many important urban cities, seriously attriting the enemy. The division's versatile tactical mobility allowed it to move expeditiously by road, air, and water to multiple besieged areas in the vicinity of Saigon and in the Delta, where the fire power and fighting spirit of the troops defeated the enemy. The distance from Xuan Loc to Can Tho was almost 200 kilometers. General Westmoreland congratulated the division on its ability to react over such a large area in such a short period of time.

The VC's disregard for the Lunar New Year Holidays, the severe property damage, and the loss of innocent civilian lives greatly alienated the people of South Vietnam from the Communists—they had expected a general uprising of the people, but it did not materialize. The Tet Offensive was a major Communist military failure, although it turned out to be a psychological victory in the realm of world opinion.

GVN Force Expansion

There were several major ramifications resulting from Tet. The Viet Cong main force units lost a great number of troops and equipment, requiring them to withdraw to their base areas to recruit, refit, and resupply. The attacks on the major cities required the VC infrastructure to surface in order to support the offensive, and the VCI as well as local force units were decimated. The withdrawal of main force units and the other VC unit losses left a void in the countryside, enabling the RVNAF to expand their control outward from the major cities. Additionally, the attacks by the Communists in 1968, particularly after Tet, alienated the people (just the opposite of the effect the Communists intended), and the people asked the GVN to provide them weapons with which to defend themselves. Thus, the concept of the People Self Defense Force (PSDF) was initiated. These were local people operating in teams for the most part at the village and hamlet level. The eleven- or fourteen-person teams had two leaders and three teams of three men and sometimes a fourth team of three women whose purpose was to defend themselves and to assist the RVNAF and National Police in maintaining security. The PSDF expanded rapidly in 1968 and 1969 to over a million trained personnel who were an important factor in pacification efforts.[2]

Recognizing the necessity for additional military and paramilitary personnel to establish governmental presence in support of pacification, in 1968, the GVN began to greatly expand and upgrade its Regional and Popular Forces. These units had been made an integral part of the RVNAF and, as such, came under the U.S. support program. Not only were their ranks expanded, but their equipment was appreciably upgraded. To entice enlistments, the RF/PF were given the same pay as the ARVN. The Popular Force units operated in platoons generally within their own district, village, or hamlet, whereas the Regional Forces operating unit was a company and it was more mobile, operating within its own province. Now, in mid-1968, the GVN was better organized to expand its pacification efforts. The RF, PF, and PSDF were the forces that brought security to the local population once the Viet Cong main force military units had been neutralized, which was the responsibility of the ARVN and U.S. forces.

Second Phase of the VC/NVA General Offensive, Mini-Tet

By late February 1968, the 9th Division had successfully completed the mop-up of those VC units that had attacked the military installations and cities in the Delta. Upon arrival in South Vietnam the previous February, the division had immediately initiated the conduct of offensive operations. Its combat effectiveness throughout the one-year period culminating in the Tet counteroffensive was superb (see table 20). At this time, Maj. Gen. Julian J. Ewell replaced Major General O'Connor as the third commanding general of the 9th Infantry Division in Vietnam. Ewell was a veteran combat commander, having commanded the 501st Airborne Infantry Regiment in its victories in stopping the German Christmas Offensive at Bastogne during the Battle of the Bulge in World War II.

Late on the evening of 5 May 1968, Col. Josiah Wallace, the 9th Infantry Division artillery commander, walked into the division's Tactical Operations Center to inform those on duty that the division's radars had picked up major movements of enemy troops toward Saigon. Upon hearing this, the division commander immediately ordered a mechanized infantry company to move that night from Long An Province to reinforce the National Police in the Saigon area south of the Kinh Doc Canal, where there were major bridges leading into the city. Major General Ewell also directed the battalion commander of the 5/60 Infantry (Mech) to establish a forward command post to maintain contact with the Vietnamese 8th Precinct officials. This proved to be a timely move, because the VC were infiltrating into the outskirts of the city and the Communist General Offensive Phase 2 had been initiated.

At first light on 7 May, a battalion-sized enemy force attacked a National Police compound south of the canal between the Highway 5 and Y Bridges and the 5/60 Infantry, which was located to secure the bridges, responded to relieve the besieged headquarters. Heavy contact ensued, and the enemy withdrew to the south. Company C pursued and reestablished contact. As the extent of the conflict grew, another company from the 5/60 Infantry Battalion responded. A POW from the 2nd Independent Battalion on that day stated that the 7, 8, and 9 Companies of his battalion were in the 8th Precinct with orders to seize and occupy the area. Thus began a series of battles, spanning 7–13 May, known as the Battle of Saigon, between the elements of the 9th Division's 3rd Brigade under Col. George Benson and seven VC battalions.[3]

On 7 May, the 3/39 Infantry Battalion was airmobiled from Long An Province to the south of the Y Bridge to block Communist movements into the city. Contact was made on 8 May, and by mid-afternoon, all elements of the 3-39 Infantry Battalion were engaged. The going was difficult because it was a street-by-street operation as they rooted out the enemy. Contact continued throughout the day. As the fighting intensified, the 2/47 Mechanized Infantry Battalion was sent that night from Bearcat through Saigon to reinforce the battle, and, upon crossing the canal about dawn, the 2/47 Infantry immediately met a large enemy unit. Contact from this engagement lasted throughout the day. On 10 May, a RF/PF outpost came under attack from an enemy battalion, and two companies of the 5/60 Mechanized Infantry engaged it. Subsequently, two companies of the 6/31 Infantry were inserted behind the enemy in an attempt to surround and annihilate him. On 11 and 12 May, many small contacts in varying degrees of intensity were made, and the battle terminated on 13 May.

Initially, the VC emplaced 107 mm rockets to fire on the center of Saigon; however, our alert air cavalry took out the rocket-firing positions before most were activated. The VC subsequently took cover in the houses of the 8th Precinct, and the resulting six days of the battle were highlighted by intense house-to-house fighting. To counter the relatively heavy enemy firepower and the large number of enemy troops, the U.S. commanders felt obliged to utilize their own firepower resources to include artillery and tactical air to minimize our casualties. They did so with maximum restraint. The VC planned their attacks on Saigon down to the smallest details, as shown in the following interrogation report:

Headquarters 9th Infantry Division
APO San Francisco, 96370

AVDE-GI

The following items are extracts from 9th Infantry Division 168-88, 180001H to 162400H June 1969 and 175-88, 230001H to 232400H June 1968, and are furnished for your information.

The following information was obtained through interrogation of Nguyen Thi Be, also known as Tu Be, also known as Huynh Thi Kien, Party name Ai, who worked for the VC since 1962 as a propaganda culture indoctrination cadre of Long An Province Committee in Ba Thu Cambodia. Tu Be was arrested by Long An Tan An City Police for carrying a false ID card on 28 May 1966.

To the best of source's knowledge and according to information given to her before leaving Cambodia on 8 May 1966, the purpose of the current attack on Saigon is to bring pressure against the GVN, to occupy as much surrounding land as possible, to demonstrate to the people that they should unite and force the U.S. to leave Vietnam. The total effort is to strengthen the position of the Hanoi Government in the Paris Peace Talks.

The source traveled with the 1st Independent Battalion on 8 May 1969 which was responsible for the 8th Precinct, the 2nd Battalion was responsible for the 7th Precinct and the 5th Nha Be LF Battalion and Dong Nai Regiment were responsible for support to those units. When the source arrived in the 8th Precinct headquarters near Hisp Phuoc Village she was given a false ID card by the secretary of the 8th Precinct Headquarters, Ba Van.

She was briefed by the Commanding Officer of the 1st Battalion, Muoi Xuong who told her that her mission was to preach propaganda to the people of the Saigon 8th District when the troops of the 1st Battalion had successfully occupied it.

She remained at the Battalion Headquarters, resting until 1600 H, 8 May 1968. She was told to wear a light blue shirt with a black patch on the breast and black pants. She was directed to go to the Pham Thien Market and look for a person, male or female dressed exactly as she was. She was to ask the person, "Do you go to the market today." The reply of the person was, "The price of the newspaper is too expensive."

At 1800 H, 8 May 1968, she contacted a Miss Bay at the market. Miss Bay, a messenger for the 8th District Propaganda Section, led her to a hut where she was told she should rest until needed. Miss Bay left hurriedly, saying not to leave the hut unless discovered by ARVN or U.S. troops. If discovered she was to run into nearby foliage and evade. At 0230H, 9 May 1968 sporadic gunfire started nearby in the Pham Thien (V) area. Miss Bay returned and led source to the market place where she was met by Tu Loc, Chief of the 8th District Propaganda Section. She was told that she and approximately 30 others were to move out into Tho (V) and talk to the residents, telling them to revolt against the GVN and protest the presence of U.S. troops.

This was to take place on a signal which would be Tu Loc on a loudspeaker asking the ARVN to throw down their arms and join the NLF. Tu Loc, at approximately 0400H, stated that the plans were not going as hoped. At this time a U.S. helicopter hovered over the market area, and the propaganda team hid near the market buildings. Source stated that she observed 40–50 VC, in grey uniforms, short pants and sleeves, with name tags identifying them as members of the 1st Battalion Reconnaissance Co. At the approach of the helicopter the VC disappeared. Source thought that they took cover in houses and buildings near the market place.

At 0700H, a U.S. helicopter circled the area with loudspeakers telling the residents to flee the area so ARVN and U.S. troops could destroy the VC without injuring innocent civilians. Shortly after, firing broke out near the market place and a U.S. gunship fired at an unknown target. Source stated that she became frightened and joined refugees fleeing toward the Chu Y Bridge to return to Cambodia. She returned from Cambodia and when she arrived at the road junction to Hwy 4 and the Tan An airstrip road she was apprehended by National Police for possession of a falsified ID card.

A. Spirito
LTC, GS

Distribution:
Special[4]

A number of prisoners were captured. The soldiers of the Phu Loi Battalion were all NVA, and each wore a tattoo on an arm, which read, "Born in the North, Die in the South." The 2nd Independent Battalion and the 6th VC Battalion had orders to attack the Y Bridge. The 3rd Brigade captured a detailed map of the area, which showed their objective as the Y Bridge. The VC often prepared after-action reports in the form of a map to critique their combat performance and determine ways to counter Allied combat techniques. We captured a goodly number of these maps (see page 104). Throughout the conflict both the NVA/VC and U.S. forces constantly adjusted their operations in order to counter opposition tactics.

Seven VC battalions were identified as participating in the attack, three of which had at least 50 percent NVA personnel. The total strength of the seven battalions was estimated to be 2,200 troops. During the period of prolonged fighting, the VC elements lost 976 killed (body count), and the United States had 305 casualties, of which 40 were killed in hostile action. Unfortunately, there were civilian casualties due to the house-to-house fighting, and the incendiary effects of the weapons firing caused very many of the wooden Vietnamese

Fig. 3. The Battle of Saigon

houses to catch fire, the flames spread by higher-than-normal winds. Nevertheless, the second phase of the Communist General Offensive against Saigon had been stopped cold in its tracks. The 9th Division had defeated most of the VC attack battalions in the environs, well short of entering Saigon.

The net effect of the tremendous losses the VC took during the Tet and Mini-Tet Offensives was to drive the VC units everywhere to ground. The Communist units generally retreated to their base areas to regroup and to rebuild, avoiding contact and fighting only when cornered. In reality, the backs of the VC units had been broken, and this ushered in a new situation in COSVN, in which unit replacements were often filled by infiltrating NVA troops.

The Communist Party Central Committees admitted that they committed an error in strategy, having launched the two abortive offenses without careful preparation.[5] Although soundly defeated, the Communists recognized that they had gained political capital, and they went about preparing for additional major offensives. Thus, the 9th Division's problem became the necessity of finding the evasive enemy units and bringing them to battle, thereby blunting enemy efforts to conduct major offensives. This required a new set of tactics differing from those when the Communists carried the battle to the Allied Forces.

Chapter 3

Enhancing Combat Capabilities

In mid-May 1968, the 9th Division found itself still responsible for a huge tactical area of responsibility that included all or parts of eight Vietnamese provinces. The division headquarters was split between Bearcat and Dong Tam, with the majority of divisional support troops and several combat battalions located at Bearcat, which was several hours by road from Dong Tam and required traveling through the built-up areas of Saigon. Also, higher headquarters had directed the division to assume several static defensive ground missions, such as defending a key signal relay site, protecting the major petroleum tank farm, and protecting highways and key bridges. The huge perimeter of Dong Tam had to be guarded while construction was ongoing. Not only that, but in combating the two phases of the VC/NVA General Offensive (Tet and Mini-Tet), the 9th Division combat units had suffered 4,458 casualties overall, which had not been totally replaced. All of the above was sapping the division's ability to perform offensive operations. The result at the time was that the infantry companies operated offensively about 50 percent of the time, with an average strength of about eighty riflemen in the field. Consequently, there were only about a thousand infantrymen operating on a daily basis.

After Mini-Tet, with the Viet Cong in the Delta highly dispersed in their base areas avoiding contact, it was going to take all the division's resources to literally beat the bushes to locate and defeat the enemy. To that end, the division required every available infantryman operating in the paddies. It was obvious what had to be done for the division to build upon its experience to date and sharpen its combat edge. Consequently, the division initiated two important, concurrent efforts to enhance its operational capabilities. The first was to ensure that the maximum number of well-supported, healthy infantrymen were available and utilized on daily combat operations. The second was to fine-tune and adjust techniques and tactics to make U.S. infantrymen as efficient as possible in the performance of operations by attriting the enemy while insuring the safety and well-being of U.S. troops.

Accomplishing these two efforts to enhance combat operations entailed deliberate, iterative procedures that required much analysis and many trials. It took over eight months for the division's operational effectiveness to peak, which it did in the period following January 1969, during the IV Corps Dry Weather Campaign, whose objective was to make an all-out push during the dry season in the Delta to crush the Communist insurgency and accelerate pacification. What follows is a discussion of the many steps taken to enhance the combat capabilities of the 9th Infantry Division.

Optimizing the Availability of the Infantry Soldier

The primary asset of an infantry division is the infantryman himself. He is the cutting edge. Therefore, the initial concentration was to take those steps necessary to have the maximum number of well-supported, healthy infantry soldiers operating in the rice paddies on a daily basis. There were never enough infantrymen to perform all the tasks in such a large area of responsibility, so the division had to optimize the availability of this vital asset. This called for two things: first, to have the maximum number of infantry companies operating offensively on a daily basis, and, second, to have those operating companies with a full complement of healthy infantrymen. That required several organizational enhancements and unit management and personnel actions.

Organizational Enhancements

Several organizational changes that would materially increase the number of infantry rifle companies in the division were ongoing or planned. The 9th Infantry Division rotated to Vietnam with seven infantry battalions, two mechanized battalions, and an armored cavalry squadron. With the division programmed to operate in the Delta, it was questionable whether the mechanized units would be effective in the inundated terrain. In early 1968, the cavalry squadron, the 3rd Squadron/5th Cavalry, was ordered to northern I Corps near the Demilitarized Zone (DMZ) to provide more armored capability because of the sizeable enemy armored threat in the vicinity. Happily, the cavalry squadron's air cavalry troop and its vital helicopter assets remained with the division. Shortly thereafter, perhaps because of the transfer of the 3rd Squadron/5th Cavalry, a new four-company rifle battalion, the 6th Battalion/31st Infantry, was assigned to the 9th Division, bringing the total number of infantry battalions to ten.

Earlier, when the VC had concentrated its efforts on interdicting the road networks by setting up ambushes to disrupt traffic, the two 9th Division mechanized battalions were extremely valuable patrolling the highways. But as the enemy went to ground, avoiding combat except for sporadic high points, the mechanized patrols were not as necessary. Then, with the division's move to the Delta, the armored personnel vehicles could be used only with extreme difficulty in the wet season and were limited even in the dry season because the terrain and the numerous blown bridges caused maneuverability difficulties. However, in built-up areas, the mechanized infantry operated well, as was exemplified by the forced march of both mechanized battalions during the Mini-Tet Offensive when they clobbered the VC and prevented its entry into the central areas of Saigon. It was obvious that the division needed more rifle infantry, and it was fortunate to be able to trade one of its mechanized battalions for a regular rifle battalion with another division whose area of operations was more suited to mechanized operations.

The 9th Division was organized at Fort Riley with three-company rifle battalions. The question of whether infantry rifle battalions in Vietnam should be organized with three or four companies was an important one. An earlier study conducted for MACV Headquarters had recommended that the optimal organization of combat in Vietnam was a four-company rifle battalion. The 9th Division experience to date indicated that it was difficult to keep a constant pressure on the enemy with a three-company battalion. This was verified later when the division determined that to prevent foot disease, troops could not operate in the inundated rice paddies for longer than forty-eight hours, which required the equivalent of one company to be always drying out. Unquestionably, a four-company battalion provided much more flexibility in operations, particularly when attempting to keep a constant night and day pressure on the enemy. Others had understood the desirability of the four-company organizational concept, and higher headquarters had approved the 9th Division conversion program of three- to four-company infantry battalions, which was almost completed by the end of the year.

The aforementioned improvements materially enhanced the division's organizational structure. From an initial posture of seven rifle battalions and two mechanized battalions with three companies each, totaling twenty-seven infantry companies, the organization had, by the end of 1968, nine infantry battalions of four companies and one mechanized battalion of three companies, for a total of thirty-nine infantry companies, a 44 percent increase in company units, which provided much greater combat flexibility and more infantrymen available for operations.

Relief from Static Missions

In late June, the construction of the 12,500-man cantonment at Dong Tam had progressed sufficiently to enable the division headquarters and the divisional units located at Bearcat to relocate to Dong Tam. This had many important salutary effects. Command was facilitated, communications improved, duplicative efforts terminated, coordination was more easily effected, support troops were two hours closer to the supported units, and the extended tactical area of responsibility (TAOR) was greatly reduced, from eight widely spread provinces to four contiguous provinces in the Upper Delta, enabling those static missions outside of the new TAOR to be dropped (see map 1). Additionally, the support troops took over from the combat units all the responsibilities for Dong Tam perimeter defenses. Then, at about the same time, as a result of the GVN's upgrading and improvements, the Regional Forces (RF) and Popular Forces (PF) capabilities improved to the extent that they were either able to directly take over some of the division's missions or they replaced ARVN infantry troops who then assumed our responsibilities. For example, on 1 July 1968, local RF/PF elements assumed the highway security mission. Eventually, as security improved, the remaining static missions were terminated, no longer necessary. So after several months, all the static missions had been terminated and the combat units of the division were able to concentrate totally on offensive operations.

Fig. 4. The Dong Tam base camp

Unit Operations

Several actions were taken to increase the number of infantry companies operating in the field on a daily basis. It was noted that the operations of the 2nd Brigade, the Mobile Riverine Force, were episodic, with about six operations per month. For that reason, in July 1968, one battalion of the 2nd Brigade was ordered to establish a base camp and to operate continuously in Kien Hoa Province to keep pressure on the enemy and by its presence to facilitate pacification efforts. Kien Hoa was the birthplace of the National Liberation Front (Viet Cong movement), and the populated province was the major source of VC recruits. At the time, this major VC stronghold had ten times as many hamlets under its control as were under GVN control. Subsequently, in January 1969, when IV Corps provided additional aviation assets, all battalions of the 2nd Brigade concentrated solely on Kien Hoa. With all battalions on the ground applying constant pressure, the operational results of the 2nd Brigade soared. It attacked base areas in the heart of Viet Cong territory, stunning and eliminating the enemy.

Additionally, the division set as a goal that the four company rifle battalions should operate daily with three companies in the field. This required excellent management of unit resources, but after a short period, almost all the rifle battalions were meeting the goal, operating both night and day. In January, after the four-company conversions were completed, nearly 75 percent of the infantry companies were operating offensively on a daily basis.

Increasing Paddy Strength

Concurrently with the unit actions, the division took steps to get more infantrymen in the field. The first step was to cut back the division headquarters units that, not surprisingly, were way over strength because of the necessity for having elements at both Bearcat and Dong Tam. It was expected that most of the over-strength personnel would be support troops, and it was surprising to find that there were many infantrymen in the headquarters, most of them with medical disabilities, generally foot problems, which prevented them from operating in the inundated rice paddies and swamps. This alerted us to the seriousness of dermatological problems. Those men who were unable to function in a rifle company counted against the division's allocation of infantrymen, so we had to find them a home with units outside the division, where they would not have to operate in water. That took some time. The division headquarters' overhead was reduced by 50 percent, and then we concentrated on reducing the size of the brigade and battalion headquarters, whose over-strengths were almost entirely infantrymen. After several attempts to get a handle on the problem, it became obvious that the solution lay in monitoring the infantry company paddy strengths, that is, the infantrymen operating in the field. After the situation had been thoroughly analyzed, we arrived at the conclusion that the optimum infantry company paddy strength should be at least 120 physically fit soldiers, or 73 percent of the 164-man authorized strength. What was required was a procedure that all units could understand and relate to. The solution was simple and very effective. Each infantry company was required to report through channels to division headquarters on a daily basis, a format that included three items: its assigned strength, the present-for-duty strength, and, of course, the paddy strength.

Recognizing that every company's situation was different—for example, some were located at small fire support bases, others were based at Dong Tam, some had just had combat casualties, et cetera—flexibility was required. General guidelines were that 10 percent of the unit could be on leave, temporary duty, or diverted to brigade or battalion headquarters, that is, not present for duty. An additional 15 percent could be on company overheads, or on general duty, sick call, or physically profiled. The temporary shortages of assigned infantrymen resulting from the Tet and Mini-Tet Communist Offensives had by July been filled, and the assigned strength of infantry companies rarely fell more than three or four personnel from the authorized strength. Thus, the units had some flexibility in the assignment of their personnel, but the paddy strength had to be at least 120 healthy infantrymen.

Operation Safe Step

Having been alerted earlier to the problem of skin diseases, the division headquarters again, in the analyses of paddy strengths, noted that there were a great number of infantrymen on sick call or carrying permanent profiles with disabilities precluding them from field duty. The primary cause of the nonavailability was severe foot problems resulting from extended periods of walking in the brackish water and constant mud. We attempted to have these men with permanent physical profiles transferred to other USARV units. Obviously, this significant loss of manpower due to these dermatological problems had to be reduced, and the division initiated Operation Safe Step, a full-court press to solve the problem, whose purpose was to control and minimize foot problems.

Upon investigation, we found that historically other armies operating in Southeast Asia had encountered the same situation. For both the British in Malaysia and the French in Indochina, the largest single cause of hospital admissions was skin disease. From July through December 1968, 55 percent of the combat man-days lost by the 9th Division maneuver battalions for all medical and surgical reasons were for dermatological treatment.

Division Surgeon Col. A. W. McFadden was given the responsibility to study this complex medical problem and hopefully to come up with a quick fix. It was obvious that only infantrymen, those who were constantly in the inundated terrain of the Mekong Delta, developed these severely incapacitating foot diseases. McFadden called upon outside help to attack the problem.

The U.S. Army Laboratory in Natick tried imaginative variations of footwear for the Mekong Delta in an effort to decrease the skin and foot problems. The division found that nylon boot socks reduced skin disease markedly more than the current issue wool socks, since they were quick-drying and comfortable, thus gaining troop acceptance. However, none of the tested experimental boots were suitable for use in the Mekong Delta.

Two stateside dermatology experts, Col. W. A. Akers and Professor David Taplan, conducted experimental research with our division surgeon to determine the effects of prolonged exposure to the Delta water. About a hundred infantrymen over a several-month period volunteered for exposure in the paddy water. The volunteers included new replacements and veteran soldiers with many months of previous exposure, including those with and without skin problems and some recently recovered from skin diseases. The experiments were conducted in rice paddies and swamp areas within the Dong Tam Base, duplicating the inundated terrain without combat exposure. Three different diseases were identified through these investigations and practical research: fungal infection, bacterial infection, and immersion foot, which was the most debilitating.

Immersion foot inevitably developed in almost all personnel exposed to prolonged periods in the muck of the Delta while wearing the standard tropical boots and wool-cushioned socks. Initially, a soldier's foot would swell and become white in appearance. Then, with walking, top layers of skin would rub off at boot contact points. No medicine could treat immersion foot. The best remedy was rest and wearing sandals while in base camp. Operation Safe Step studies indicated that after two days in the rice paddies, a unit could become 50 percent or more disabled, and the problem increased greatly with longer periods of water exposure. However, immersion foot could be almost completely avoided by limiting soldiers' exposure in the field to forty-eight hours. The first symptoms of fungal disease normally did not appear until after forty-eight hours in the paddies, although it could be treated by an antibiotic. There are always bacteria on the skin, and bacteria thrived in the heat and humidity of Vietnam. Thus, any minor break of the skin could cause infections. No really effective solution was found to prevent or to treat bacterial skin infections.

Thus, the major finding of Operation Safe Step was that normal healthy skin can tolerate about forty-eight hours of continuous exposure to paddy water before developing immersion foot syndrome or fungal diseases. Consequently, on 28 October 1968 a directive was issued limiting combat operations to forty-eight hours except for real tactical emergencies, followed by a twenty-four-hour drying out period.[1] One may ask why the indigenous rice farmers rarely developed the condition. The answer is simply that they went barefoot or wore sandals and they had opportunities to dry out, particularly at night.

The practical medical research of Operation Safe Step was undoubtedly unique for a combat division in the field. This command-supported initiative did much to ensure that, by following the time limitations on combat duty in the field, the division had healthy soldiers in the field. It was a major factor in allowing unit commanders to meet their paddy-strength requirement.

Decades later, two medical specialists writing in professional papers have cited Operation Safe Step for its effectiveness in reducing dermatological disease, concluding: "The story of the 9th Infantry underscores at least three preventive medicine themes. First, surveillance data is invaluable, both in identifying problems and in guiding toward solutions. Second, medical research is not only possible but can be extremely useful, *even when deployed*. Finally, command emphasis is central to prevention of disease and non-battle injury."[2]

Tiger Scouts

The GVN established the Chieu Hoi (Open Arms) Program to entice Communists to leave the VC and rally to the government's side. Ralliers, called Hoi Chanhs, underwent several months of reeducation at Chieu Hoi centers, and upon their release, they were eligible for employment on the economy or with GVN or U.S. government agencies, if they so desired. The U.S. Armed Forces hired many of them. The pay of the Hoi Chanhs had to be budgeted so that their utilization by military units was controlled. The 9th Division found the Hoi Chanhs, which it called "Tiger Scouts," a real combat asset and fully used its 250-person authorization, integrating them directly into infantry units. Some other units didn't.

Fig. 5. Stream-crossing in Long An Province

Another personnel step the division took to improve the paddy strength was to obtain an increase in the authorization for Tiger Scouts from 250 to 400 personnel, the goal being to assign one Tiger Scout to each infantry squad. These defectors, having deserted, were generally strongly anti-Communist. The Tiger Scouts' knowledge of the local terrain, their familiarity with enemy tactics, and their ability to communicate with the Vietnamese people made them invaluable assets.

Their ability to solicit information from prisoners and the local population alike was extremely useful. We found the Tiger Scouts very loyal once they had been integrated into a unit. They rarely deserted or were suspected of being disloyal. After a short period, they could generally communicate with the soldiers. The Tiger Scout program was successful in that it increased our paddy strength by more than 10 percent and facilitated operations in the Vietnamese environment. The Tiger Scouts were very brave and valued members of the infantry units, particularly in ferreting out the enemy, as this example of an action by the 4/47 Infantry Battalion on 21 March 1969 indicates:

> Action began just as night fell and Company A was moving into a night position following a daytime sweep of an area believed to be the base for fifty to sixty Viet Cong. A Tiger Scout assigned to 3rd Platoon spotted three enemy soldiers and engaged them, whereupon the enemy retaliated with grenades, mortars and rockets. It became suddenly apparent that the whole company was in an L-shaped ambush and was taking fire from three sides. The enemy then launched suicidal attacks with human waves. The Company Commander quickly adjusted artillery fire and directed gunships onto the attackers, catching them in the open. The withering fire soon caused the attacks to subside and left 40 dead enemy strewn about the battlefield. Friendly losses were only one killed and nine wounded. Said one of the U.S. soldiers, "That night was worse than any movie I've ever seen. The enemy charged right up to our positions and threw grenades, but we finally beat them back. It was pretty near daylight before any of us got any sleep out there in the mud."

A New Tactical Area of Responsibility

With the move to Dong Tam, the division's tactical area of responsibility was reduced so that it now included four large provinces: Long An and Dinh Tuong, for which it had responsibility previously, plus Kien Hoa and Go Cong. Long An was situated in Southwestern III Corps Tactical Zone while the other three provinces were located in northeastern IV Corps Tactical Zone. All the provinces were in the Delta region of South Vietnam. Long An abutted the Capitol Military District in the south; Dinh Tuong was one of the wealthiest provinces and controlled the main communications route from Saigon to the Delta; and Kien Hoa was the birthplace of the Viet Cong movement

Enhancing Combat Capabilities 33

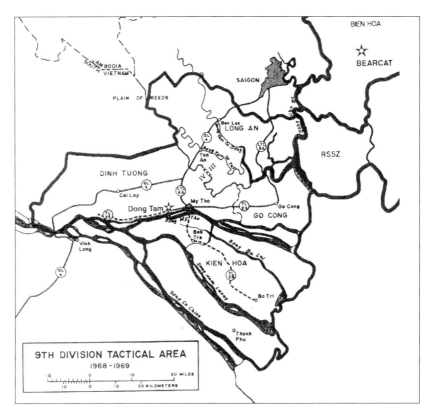

Map 1. 9th Infantry Division tactical area of responsibility, 31 August 1968

and was a hotbed of Communist activities. In July 1968, these three provinces had less than 20 percent of their population securely under the control of the GVN, whereas Go Cong was a more secure province, allowing the division to concentrate offensive operations in the other three. All of the four were relatively highly populated, and their total number of inhabitants was about 1,800,000, of which 80 percent were living in 1,720 small rural hamlets and were mostly farmers.

All of the provinces in the 9th Division TAOR were within the COSVN's Second Military Region, which included the area south and west of Saigon. Thus, the Viet Cong military activities were generally centrally controlled and coordinated. The Viet Cong Base Area 470 encompassed an area of approximately 450 square kilometers in western Dinh Tuong Province, extending into both Kien Tuong and Kien

Fig. 6. A Tiger Scout

Phong Provinces. At the time, the NVA were utilizing the Cambodian port of Kampong Som, and a main supply route for infiltrating supplies to the upper Delta went directly to Base Area 470. Kien Hoa and Long An Communist units each also had a major base area where the Viet Cong conducted training, logistics, and resupply and staged for combat operations. For several years, the base areas had been almost sacrosanct from attack by the RVNAF. The so-called Parrot's Beak in

Cambodia, protected by the Plain of Reeds, pointed directly toward the 9th Division TAOR and was the origin of a continuous flow of material and combatants into the upper Delta.

The main communications route in the TAOR was Highway QL-4, which ran from Saigon through Long An and Dinh Tuong Provinces to the lower Delta. It was the lifeline of commerce connecting the capitol to the lush rice basket of South Vietnam, and because of its vital importance it was called the "People's Road." Keeping this busy highway open and cleared was of paramount importance. General Westmoreland had a personal interest in the matter and had discussed the significance on several occasions with the division commander. The VC understood that if the populated Delta could not transport its goods to Saigon, morale would be greatly affected. Therefore, they constantly attempted to mine the road, establish ambushes, and blow up the two main bridges at Tan An and Ben Luc in Long An Province. Other key roads were TL-24, connecting My Tho City with Go Cong City; LTL-5A, connecting Go Cong City with Saigon, which was little used because of bridge destruction; and TL-26, the major route in Kien Hoa connecting the provincial capital Ben Tre City with Ba Tri City. Additionally, there were numerous small roads connecting the hundreds of hamlets with major villages, the so-called farm-to-market routes that were so essential in keeping the rural economy vibrant. A major mission, obviously, was to keep these lines of commerce open, because if pacification was to proceed, the farmers required not only the security of their hamlets but also the ability to market their crops.

The Results

Initially, the division was organized with twenty-seven rifle companies (excluding the cavalry squadron). In mid-May, many of these units were tied down by assigned static defensive missions. Other units were operating episodically. A large number of infantrymen had incapacitating foot problems. Overall, there were not more than a thousand infantrymen operating on a daily basis. By January 1969, the rifle battalions had been converted from three to four companies, providing much greater flexibility, and, as the result of other organizational refinements, there were thirty-nine infantry companies; all static defensive requirements had been terminated; the debilitating foot problem had been solved; there was one Tiger Scout per infantry squad; the infantry companies were regularly meeting the paddy strength quota of at least 120 men; and rifle battalions were operating daily with three companies in the field. Thus, the division had over 3,500 infantrymen aggressively pursuing the enemy night and day, a manifold increase in the cutting edge of divisional operations.

To ensure that these infantrymen were well supported in the Delta environment, it was absolutely essential to operations that they be accompanied by the maximum number of aviation assets and be provided with outstanding combat intelligence to improve their tactical success and to minimize casualties. These two key support elements, the optimization of aviation assets and the integration of intelligence with operations, are discussed subsequently.

Optimizing Helicopter Assets

The main advantages—other than the leadership, training, and spirit of our troops—that the Americans had over the Communists were our firepower and mobility. With respect to firepower, the infantrymen were supported by artillery, tactical air, and helicopter gunships. The division always ensured that the infantrymen had artillery fire support. The riverine force designed and fabricated six barges, each capable of carrying two 105 mm howitzers that were towed wherever the Navy craft transported our waterborne troops. To ensure that artillery could always support the soldiers operating in the muck and water of the Delta, artillery-firing platforms capable of being airlifted by CH-47 helicopters were built. Each platform supported a 105 mm howitzer and had four adjustable legs with broad feet, enabling it to be stabilized and leveled while sitting in the rice paddies.

The Air Force had forward air controllers (FAC) assigned to the division; these would direct the high performance aircraft in their bombing runs. Air Force support was superb, particularly in our "seal and pile-on" operations, when we used our great firepower to attack the enemy. We usually requested preplanned Air Force sorties, which were capable of being diverted by the FACs to contact locations if necessary; for example:

Fig. 7. Relocating artillery

Airmobile operations were conducted on 6 February 1969 by elements of the 2nd Brigade, near the "Crossroads," south of Dong Tam and near Mo Cay, which accounted for sixteen enemy dead. Soon after inserting in the vicinity of Mo Cay, the men of 3/60 Infantry came in contact with an enemy force of unknown size. One enemy was killed immediately by the ground forces and air strikes by F-100 fighters were called in. The jets destroyed sixteen structures and seven enemy bunkers, causing two large secondary explosions that sent white smoke billowing more than a thousand feet in the air. On the heels of the air strikes, the infantrymen swept the area, and five enemy soldiers were dislodged from a bunker and captured.

However, the most important sources of firepower were the gunships of the air cavalry troops (ACT) and the helicopters of the assault helicopter companies (AHC). These helicopters accompanied the troops in airmobile operations and were available when troops on the ground needed assistance. Not only did the helicopters provide firepower, but in the inundated Delta, with its poor road system, they were the primary source of troop-carrying mobility as well as reconnaissance. Consequently, the division took all possible steps to ensure that the troops in the field had optimal aircraft support, since the Mekong Delta combat capability was directly correlated with Army aviation assets. The assault helicopter companies greatly enhanced maneuverability and the air cavalry troops, with their rockets and mini-guns, provided on-the-spot firepower as well as reconnaissance capabilities. Because aviation support was so critical to tactical success, we carefully analyzed all aspects of Army aviation assets to include combat effectiveness, availability, utilization, allocations, and tactics in order to maximize capabilities.

Aircraft Combat Effectiveness

It was obvious in the Delta terrain that aviation assets were vital to combat effectiveness. The problem was there were never enough assets to support each brigade. At the time, an ACT was available 50 percent of the time and an AHC 65 percent of the time. The question was how should the assets be utilized for the maximum combat effectiveness? For example, some commanders used both the ACT and AHC together in support of a unit. Others divided the assets; the ACT supported one unit and the AHC the other. It was important to determine the effectiveness of aviation asset utilization.

We successively brought several first-class officers into the Command Section to study those areas affecting combat operations which lent themselves to systematic analysis, such as aircraft utilization. These outstanding officers were Maj. Edwin A. Deagle Jr., Maj. John O. B. Sewell, and Maj. Jack O. Bradshaw. Deagle and Sewell summarized the division's tactical operations and concepts, and Deagle conducted a study concerning improvements in combat efficiency resulting from the utilization of aviation assets.[3] Since our division objective was to find and destroy the enemy, the analysis focused on enemy contacts and attrition. The assets studied were the utilization of assault helicopter companies and air cavalry troops; since it was divisional policy to give commanders maximum control of their combat assets, these were allocated to brigades on a daily basis and put under their operational control. Consequently, the brigade was used as the basic maneuver unit in measuring the results of aviation assets upon combat operational effectiveness.

Deagle's study initially focused on the 1st Brigade operations in Dinh Tuong Province between 7 March and 22 June 1968, and the 3rd Brigade operations in Long An and Gia Dinh Provinces between 1 March and 6 May 1968.[4] When he had collated his data, the results were so surprising that we immediately passed the word to the brigades. Initial results indicated that ten times as many VC were eliminated when both an ACT and AHC were utilized jointly than when no assets were available, and the combined utilization was several times more effective than if an AHC or an ACT was solely operating in support. To complete his study, Major Deagle then analyzed the results of the 1st, 2nd, and 3rd Brigade operations between 1 July and 15 August 1968. During this period, the 1st Brigade utilized both the AHC and ACT operating together on every occasion when it had both aircraft assets with great results. Deagle's study included a total of 313 brigade days of combat, from 1 March through 15 August 1968. This period was prior to the increases in paddy strengths and before we had perfected our tactical innovations, yet the results were definitely meaningful. With no airmobile or air cavalry support, the three brigades averaged 0.21 significant enemy contacts per day. When supported by either an assault helicopter company or an air cavalry troop, the number of contacts did not improve significantly. However, when supported by both companies, the number of enemy contacts increased to 0.49 per day, or one significant contact every other day. When the Viet Cong losses were considered, the brigade output averaged 1.6 Viet Cong losses per day with no aviation assets and increased to between 5 and 6 Viet Cong losses per day when only one of the helicopter companies was utilized. Thus, although there was no increase in the number of contacts, the

Table 1. 9th Infantry Division aircraft combat effectiveness,
1 March–15 August 1968

Ground forces	Total VC significant contacts	Total VC losses per day	Total U.S. casualties per contact	VC losses versus U.S. KHA
With no air assets	0.21	1.6	14.1	8.2
With an air cavalry troop only	0.23	5.1	14.4	10.5
With an assault helicopter company only	0.21	6.0	17.1	10.1
With both an air cavalry troop and an assault helicopter company	0.49	13.6	11.2	12.9

Source: Edwin A. Deagle, Staff Study: Utilization of Non-Organic Aviation Assets. Headquarters, 9th Infantry Division, Republic of Vietnam, 1968.

number of enemy eliminated increased three times with the utilization of one of the air assets. However, when a brigade was supported by both an assault helicopter company and an air cavalry troop, the results increased strikingly to 13.6 Viet Cong eliminated daily, an 850 percent improvement over the situation with no helicopter assets.

Since it was always the goal of the 9th Infantry Division to maximize our capabilities to destroy the enemy while at the same time minimizing our own personnel losses, the ratio of enemy eliminated to friendly killed was considered an excellent measure of combat effectiveness. Under all conditions, the maneuver forces were highly combat effective. With no assets, the ratio of enemy losses to U.S. soldiers killed by hostile action was 8.2 to 1, and it increased to 10.3 and 10.5 with only one helicopter asset, and jumped to 12.9 with both helicopter assets in support. But what was more important, the total number of casualties (killed and wounded) per contact was less when both assets were involved. This reduction in the number of U.S. casualties is not too surprising, considering that the great increase in observation, maneuverability, and firepower made combat operations much more effective, thereby protecting the troops.

At this time, before the division perfected its tactics, the marshy swamps and inundated rice paddies of the Delta terrain made it very difficult to contact and to eliminate the enemy by ground maneuvers. On the other hand, the open, flat countryside was ideal terrain for the employment of Army Aviation. Because of the improvement in combat effectiveness and the reduced casualty rate, we went all-out to increase the availability and utilization of air assets. Subsequently, when the division's innovative maneuvers and aviation tactics had been developed, the combat effectiveness improved even more.

Aircraft Availability

Although the 9th Division relied heavily on the outside aviation support provided by II Field Force, we also could not operate effectively without the organic aviation assets—that is, equipment of the division, not from outside units—in our two operational units, D Troop, 3rd Battalion, 5th Cavalry and A Company, 9th Aviation Battalion. So we set about to optimize the availability of their helicopters, that is, to have the maximum number of aircraft operationally available on a daily basis. To accomplish this, we had to improve our aircraft maintenance. Therefore, we formalized an aircraft maintenance program. We centralized the responsibility for the maintenance of all divisional aviation assets under the division aviation officer. To facilitate the maintenance tasks, we distributed the aviation assets so as to have, as far as possible, only a single type of aircraft assigned to each unit. Having done that, we decentralized maintenance by authorizing our two operational units to perform their own third-echelon maintenance. The attached B Company, 709th Maintenance Battalion, which did a great job, performed all other maintenance. Then we established an inviolate weekly stand-down for each aircraft. We had found that operational requirements often overrode maintenance procedures and that the aircraft were not undergoing timely periodic inspections. The stand-down really paid off because it enabled maintenance to be performed on minor items before they became major problems. Since the majority of our organic assets were utilized in daytime operations, we initiated night maintenance. In November 1968, adequate maintenance hangars were finally completed at Dong Tam, and the lights in those hangars burned all night every night. Our mechanics had high morale, and they took pride in ensuring that our aircraft were operationally ready. As much as anyone, they were responsible for the improvements in combat effectiveness.

However, all the organizational refinements, facility improvements, and esprit of personnel would amount to naught if our mechanics did not have the necessary repair parts on hand to maintain the aircraft. The division spent a great amount of time and effort trying to coax repair parts out of a reluctant system. We requisitioned according to the manuals, stationed a sharp noncommissioned officer at the depot to monitor our requisitions, and had daily special runs to pick up available parts. Critical aviation repair parts were of vital interest at all echelons, from the Pentagon down to the units, and by working together, the system produced for us.

With constant command attention (the division aircraft maintenance officer reported to me every night at 2000 hrs to review aircraft status), by the end of 1968 we had raised aircraft availability from around 50 percent to consistently above 80 percent. This provided the division much greater flexibility, particularly in our ability to support innovative night tactics.

Aircraft Utilization

Initially, we focused on the availability of aircraft, concentrating on maintenance. However, that was only one side of the coin, the other being the utilization of the helicopter assets. We counted on at least 70 percent of our aircraft being operationally ready on a daily basis. The question was, considering our tactical techniques, what was a reasonable level of utilization for both helicopters and pilots? To determine the answer, we did a thorough analysis of both organic and allocated aircraft. Considering all aspects of tactical operations, the average requirements for the five various types of aircraft in the air cavalry troops, the assault helicopter companies, and organic aviation units varied in a range between 98 and 105 hours per month per aircraft. We then accepted 100 hours per aircraft per month as a standard utilization factor. The U.S. Army Vietnam utilization average was 67 hours per month, so the 9th Division utilization standard was 50 percent greater.[5] With this, we found that the average number of pilot hours per month for the five types of helicopter assets varied between 60 and

103, well below the 140-hour maximum stipulated by regulations. We wanted our pilots to be as fresh and alert as possible.[6]

Another aspect of utilization was the aircraft basing. Prior to December 1968, the allocated support aircraft would have to deadhead from their bases outside the division area to and from our brigade locations. This took valuable flying hours. However, in December, both organic and support aircraft moved to Dong Tam, which was central in our area of operations, thus saving valuable flying hours. Another unproductive deadhead was the requirement for operational helicopters to refuel and/or rearm. So, to reduce the necessity of returning to Dong Tam, we established refueling and rearming locations at outlying base camps. These actions increased productive aircraft utilization by about 25 percent.

Last, we aggressively managed our aircraft assets. We established within our divisional tactical operations center an organization responsible for controlling every aircraft, both organic and attached, at all times. We called this our air control team. It enabled the division to react swiftly and effectively to new enemy intelligence and operational requirements. Generally, no aircraft was held in reserve or on daytime standby, because we had the ability to divert immediately as required.

We did everything possible to ensure that every available flying hour was utilized on tactical operations to find and defeat the enemy.

Aircraft Allocations

The preponderance of our tactical aviation support was allocated to the division by higher headquarters. Consequently, our combat efficiency was in large measure a function of those allocations. During the latter part of 1968, II Field Force generally allocated the division two assault helicopter companies and one air cavalry troop. Considering maintenance stand-downs and diversions to other II Field Force units, this averaged about fifty-three assault helicopter company days per month and twenty-two air cavalry troop days per month. Considering our own organic air cavalry, we had about forty-eight air cavalry days per month. With three brigades constantly in the field, that meant that every day at least one brigade had no air assets; consequently, there was always a requirement to allocate helicopter assets. The allocation was a function of the intelligence picture, since the division was always

Fig. 8. The critical trooper—helicopter mechanic

focused on finding and destroying the enemy. The two brigades with the most promising opportunities received the aviation assets.

Aviation Tactics

Since the Viet Cong in our sector of operations had broken down into small groups and were avoiding combat, our airmobile tactics following the USARV doctrine that required that airmobile assaults be conducted by ten helicopters covered by two light-fire teams of four gunships were proving unwieldy. We desired to break down into smaller assault units to enable air assets to cover a larger area, thus keeping greater pressure on the enemy. We took the matter personally to 1st Aviation Brigade Commander Maj. Gen. Robert Williams, who often monitored 9th Division contacts, requesting authority to utilize five slick insertions covered by one light-fire team. He gave us permission to do so on a trial basis. The effect of breaking down into smaller assault groups was dramatic, since it enabled us to check out twice as many intelligence targets, doubling the pressure on the enemy.

The conduct of the airmobile assaults was also of prime importance in obtaining results. It was customary in Vietnam to prep the helicopter landing zones with artillery fire, to reduce the amount of enemy fire against the helicopters and our ground troops. It soon became evident in the Delta area that the artillery preparatory fire alerted the enemy, allowing them often to evade our insertions. So we initiated a no-prep policy, of course with artillery standing by, should it be necessary. This greatly increased the element of surprise. At what distance from the suspected enemy positions should the helicopters insert the infantrymen? This was a major question; initially, insertions were made about six hundred meters from the target, to minimize the effects of direct fire. However, that meant that it took the troops appreciable time and effort wading through the muck of rice paddies to close in on the enemy, and the element of surprise was reduced. Subsequently, the insertion distance was cut to about three hundred meters, and we had very few problems. It was obvious that the Viet Cong were avoiding contact at all costs; a major reason was the firepower cover provided by the observation aircraft, Cobras, and gunships. Every time a Viet Cong fired his weapon, he signed his death warrant, because the helicopter picked him off unless he was in a bunker. Eventually, as the enemy attempted to stay concealed and refused to fire on our insertions until troops had closed within a dozen meters of their position, our more accomplished commanders would insert at a hundred meters or even less. These audacious assaults fixed the enemy in place, preventing his attempts to escape, and our combat results increased greatly.

Not long after we initiated our airmobile assault tactics, the Viet Cong Military Region 2, which included all of our TAOI, sent a letter to its subordinate units describing the division's airmobile tactics, which they called "Hawk Tactics." This letter, which was captured about 20 September 1968, directed the Viet Cong units to set up ambushes "in the areas where the enemy has frequently landed." The letter also pointed out several weaknesses in our tactics: first, operations were generally conducted from 0900 hours to late afternoon; second, command and control helicopters circled suspected landing zones several times before insertion; and third, the landing force was normally a small unit without support. The Viet Cong anti-Hawk tactics were effective in July and August, when thirty-one helicopters were shot down. The Division immediately issued guidance to all unit commanders specifying Hawk tactic actions to be taken to counter the VC countermeasures. Our instructions paid off: we lost two helicopters in November and only one in December.

> From: MR II Hq
> To: The Regiments
> Subject: The "Hawk Tactics" applied by US Air Cavalry Forces
> 1. The US Forces have recently been applying the "Hawk Tactic" in their operations.
> 2. They often heliborne troops and suddenly land them along communications routes or in the suburbs of cities or district sites. This tactic is used for the following reasons:
>   a) Usually the US Forces drop troops at common routes, suburbs of cities and district sites for the purpose of observing or discovering our forces. If our forces were present in or around their LZ, they tried to interfere with our operational plan or the preparing of our combat plan. They heliborne troops deep within our base sites, with the intention of detecting our camp positions or our

installations. Once having located the camp sites and installations, they continue the attack and cause disorder and damage to our base areas. They attack the "corridor area" [*sic*] causing casualties among our troops during movement and to our cadres who are operating separately.

    b) *Conspiracies:* The period during which troops were landed was not listed on the schedule—usually they landed from 0900H or 1000H and continuing until late afternoon. The enemy force consists of 3 to 5 helicopters including 1 or 2 CP choppers; the maximum strength is less than two squads.

3. They didn't prepare the LZ, the CP chopper circled several times and they landed immediately. Sometimes they dropped the troops 200–300 meters away from the edge of a village; sometimes they dropped the troops close to the edge of the village. If they detected a small force, they attacked immediately; if they discovered our large units, the enemy withdrew to the rice paddies and called for reinforcements and geared for a large operation. In a time frame of a few days, these "hawk-tactic" raiding forces can attack many different areas.

4. The enemy selected open terrain for applying the "Hawk Tactic." The advantage of this tactic was in using a small force without preparing the landing zone. They are able to attack quickly and retreat quickly —their movement is very fast. But they have a weak point, namely a small unit without support and are, therefore, easy to destroy.

5. For disrupting the enemy tactic, the chief of staff department has outlined some important points:

    a) The 2 Regiments will select several squads for training. Each squad will be armed with one AR, one claymore, 3–4 AK-47s, and one sniping rifle. These squads will linkup with local guerrillas and set up ambushes in the areas where the enemy has frequently landed. Also, we will set up ambushes in other areas.

    b) Action taken: If the enemy drops their troops close to the edge of a village, and the choppers have not quite landed, we will concentrate maximum firepower to destroy the enemy force immediately. The function of the sniping cell will be to shoot down the CP chopper.

6. If the enemy drops his troops away from the edge of the village, we will deploy in combat formations and wait for them. When they are about 3–4 meters from our positions we open fire.

7. If the enemy drops troops on our position, it depends on the situation. After we have destroyed the enemy force and cleared the battlefield, we will move to another location 300–500 meters from the contact area and deploy again, ready to fight.
8. These are several ideas which I wanted to discuss with the comrades. We will attempt to organize and research methods for countering this "Hawk Tactic." Train and try to gain more experience and report to MR II Hq on the progress being made. If anyone has any ideas on the subject, please discuss them with the Department Chief of Staff of MR II.[7]

The aforementioned was only one of the many pieces of evidence we found where the Viet Cong analyzed our tactics and proposed countermeasures to combat them. In October 1968, for example, we captured a series of maps of different battles with various Viet Cong units analyzing our airmobile and encirclement techniques. The Viet Cong were quick to catch on, and we had to be alert to their changes in tactics in order to be successful.

Noting that the Viet Cong expected our assaults to be daytime actions, we began to evolve night tactics—both ground and air. With our improved maintenance, the aircraft availability and utilization increased to the point where we were also able to use our organic air cavalry troop for night operations. This was the final major step essential to maintaining an overwhelming, constant pressure on the Viet Cong. Consequently, we were able to take the night away from the enemy, utilizing our far-ranging aircraft and the tremendous advantages that night-vision devices provided to interdict his movements of men and materiel.

Thus, by breaking down into smaller air assault units operating with lightning insertions and by utilizing our helicopter assets at night, we revolutionized airmobile operations in the Delta, allowing us to maintain a relentless and constant pressure, day and night.

The skill and courage of our pilots was outstanding, which is exemplified by this citation of WO1 (Warrant Officer, 1st Class) David G. Newkirk:

Singled out for bravery in the 4-47 Infantry action was WO1 David J. Newkirk of D/3-5 Cav, who blatantly exposed his light observation helicopter to enemy snipers in order to locate their positions. Hovering his light aircraft just above the nipa palm and using the propwash of his blades to separate the foliage, Newkirk located several snipers and silenced them with his mini-guns and grenades. Although his aircraft received numerous hits, he continued these daring tactics until all of the enemy snipers menacing the advancing riverine infantrymen had been eliminated. He then directed the infantrymen to other enemy positions he had spotted.

When the company he was supporting was unable to reach an area in the dense vegetation suitable for medical evacuation of the wounded, Newkirk volunteered to maneuver his craft through a small opening in the trees to pick up the seriously wounded. Although under enemy automatic weapons fire, the pilot skillfully lowered his helicopter, clipping the heavy foliage with both his main and tail rotors. The enemy fire intensified during the laborious loading process, but Newkirk refused to lift off until as many wounded as he could carry were aboard. After the dust-off, the steely aviator repeated the heroic action a second time. Newkirk's actions typify the helicopter pilots from every cavalry troop and assault helicopter company supporting the 9th Division. Their bravery and esprit are extraordinary and were major factors in the unprecedented success of the 9th Division's helicopter-infantry team.

Integration of Intelligence

Intelligence was the primary targeting method in support of combat operations that were at all times focused on the elimination of the enemy to include his main and local force units, guerrilla and VC infrastructure. Meaningful intelligence enabled troops to ferret out the dispersed enemy without beating the bushes, which was costly in expended effort and increased casualties resulting from the ubiquitous booby traps.

In Vietnam, there were many sources of intelligence information, both internal and external. Real-time intelligence was very important, since information generally was a perishable commodity that had to be reacted to immediately to be useful for tactical operations. However, information from all sources, when properly processed, created a mosaic that was extremely valuable in providing a "feel" of the enemy situation since the enemy was prone to follow established patterns of movement.

There were two broad sources of information: HUMINT, or intelligence obtained from personnel in the field; and sensors, which were mechanical and electronic devices. HUMINT included information obtained by our Integrated Civic Action Program, prisoners of war, Hoi Chanhs, agents, and friendly Vietnamese. Sensor information was obtained from airborne personnel detectors, unattended ground sensors, Usually Reliable Intelligence, side-looking airborne radar, airborne infrared, and ground surveillance radars. The division utilized all available intelligence sources, both internal and external, HUMINT and sensor, U.S. and Vietnamese, friendly and enemy. These sources were constantly analyzed and appraised for their reliability and usefulness. A measure of the relative reliability of intelligence was the number of confirmable reports from each source.

Between March and April 1969, the division logged an astonishing 8,172 reports received from major sources.[8] This total excluded the twenty to thirty daily sighting reports from the divisional ground surveillance radars. Of the total, 31 percent, or 2,559, were reacted to, and, of these, 28 percent, or 709, were confirmed (see table 2). Our intelligence section, under the guidance of Lt. Col. Leonard Spirito, did an outstanding job of coordinating and managing the myriad of sources and evaluating the information, thereby enabling the division to operate against valid targets. Often, reports from different sensors would be duplicated, some reports would be stale, too old to react to, and some were from sources not considered reliable. Although to the uninitiated, the 709 confirmed intelligence reports (9 percent of the overall reports) may not appear substantial, it was an excellent batting average; over ten contacts per day, or about 40 percent of the total divisional contacts during the two-month period, were targeted from intelligence sources.

The overall percentages of confirmations from HUMINT reports, at 15 percent, was just over double the percentage of confirmations obtained from sensors, at 7 percent—this even though the receipt of the HUMINT reports took an average of eighteen to seventy-two hours. It was several months after our move to the Delta in July 1968 before the G-2 could establish an agent network, but by March 1969, it was operating most effectively, with 885 agent reports received. However, the most reliable source of HUMINT came from the Vietnamese vil-

Table 2. 9th Infantry Division Reliability of Intelligence Resources, 1 March–30 April 1969

Source	Timeliness hours	Quantity received	Reactions (percent)	Confirmed (percent)	Overall confirmed (percent)
HUMINT					
Integrated Civic Action Program	24	318	147 (46)	60 (41)	19
Agent Reports	72	885	357 (40)	135 (38)	15
Prisoners of War, Hoi-Chanhs	18	367	110 (30)	42 (30)	11
Subtotal	–	1,570	514 (39)	237 (39)	15
Sensors					
Airborne personnel detector	0.2	310	207 (67)	106 (51)	34
Unattended ground sensors*	0.6	350	229 (65)	49 (21)	14
Usually Reliable Intelligence	2	1,368	193 (14)	98 (51)	7
Side-looking airborne radar	12	2,785	1,076 (39)	137 (13)	5
Airborne infrared	12	1,930	240 (13)	82 (13)	4
Subtotal	–	6,602	1,945 (29)	472 (24)	7
Total	–	8,172	2,559	709 (28)	9

Source: Lt. Leonard A. Spirito, "Reliability of Intelligence, Resources," Headquarters 9th Infantry Division, Republic of Vietnam, May 1969.
Note: *Reacted to by artillery fire only

lagers who were being medically treated by the ICAPs. Once security was established in the hamlets, the peasants were pleased to inform on the detested Communists who had previously harshly intimidated them. Generally speaking, reactions to HUMINT reports enabled us to scarf up groups of guerrillas and VCIs.

Prisoners of war and Hoi Chanhs were veritable fountains of information. An unusual facet of the Vietnam War was that captured prisoners opened up and told everything they knew. We were informed that the Viet Cong taught that anyone who was captured by the Americans would be killed; consequently they should fight to the death. As a result, when captured POWs realized they were being treated well, they opened up. The information received did not always lead to potential new contacts. For example, some stated they were short of ammunition, thereby indicating our interdiction efforts were paying off. Others said they were short of rice, leading us to believe the peasants were not as supportive as in the past. So the division strongly emphasized the desirability of obtaining POWs and Hoi Chanhs, not only for the information they conveyed but because it was certainly a humane outcome. Whenever our combat units were involved in a seal-and-pile-on operation, they would use bull horns to attempt to talk the enemy into surrendering. During March and April 1969, 240 POWs were captured. They produced more intelligence, which in turn produced more targets, which led to more POWs, and the cycle of success just grew. Every prisoner was a source of information, particularly a VC company commander who Warrant Officer Holt captured.

> Before the afternoon was over, the gunships had killed thirty-nine Viet Cong and taken nine detainees. Troops of the 6-31 Infantry added four more. Warrant Officer Mike Holt and one other gunship piloted by Lieutenant Mike Arruti flew on station for two hours until almost all their fuel and all the ammunition had been expended. Prior to departing the scene Holt and his crew captured Viet Cong company commander of the 514 C Main Force Battalion.

The division's interest in capturing prisoners was so great that in early 1969, the battalion commander of the 2/39 Infantry, upon seeing a Viet Cong fleeing into the nipa, landed to apprehend the enemy and, in so doing, was fatally shot. Lt. Col. Don Schroeder was a truly outstanding combat leader, unquestionably one of the division's best, and all sincerely mourned his death.

GVN organizations were also excellent sources of information. We worked closely with the South Vietnamese Army units in our area as well as with the National Police. Since the Vietnamese had a more thorough knowledge of the enemy, close and continuous exchanges were essential to our intelligence operations. They quickly recognized that with our aviation assets, we could respond rapidly to intelligence targets, so they became much more forthcoming in the exchange of perishable information. These close intelligence contacts led to greater cooperation in operational matters also, so that in our area, all Allied units more aggressively targeted the enemy. Overall, HUMINT was our most reliable source of intelligence information, with 39 percent of all reactions confirmed.

Although the reliability of HUMINT sources was double that of sensors, the number of confirmed reactions to sensor reports was double (472) the HUMINT (237) in the period because four times as many sensor reports were received. The reports most frequently reacted to were those received in real time, that is, the airborne personnel detector (People Sniffer) and the unattended ground sensors. The "People Sniffer" was the most reliable source, with 34 percent of all readings confirmed. Obviously, with the air cavalry on the spot, reactions were quickly made. Considering the percentage of reports reacted to, both the People Sniffer and the Usually Reliable Intelligence reports had over 50 percent confirmed. Note that there was a reporting lag time of about twelve hours for both the side-looking airborne radar (SLAR) and infrared readings. If there had been a download capability located at the division, these two sources would have been immensely more valuable. The SLAR was particularly adept at picking up enemy movements. Sensors, unlike HUMINT, often found targets of opportunity that led to major contacts where enemy units were severely mauled. This was often true when the enemy was attempting to position itself for one of its attempted highpoint attacks. The large number of sensor reports was valuable not only to react to but to portray patterns of enemy activities.

Since intelligence was the main divisional targeting device, we needed a tool for orchestrating the intelligence and operational functions. This was simply a twice-daily command and staff briefing held at 0700 and 1700 hrs. The intelligence portion of the briefing consisted of discussing significant friendly and enemy activities throughout the corps tactical zones. The focus was a graphic display of all enemy activities and reports presented on a large-scale map, which contained all activities reported in the past seventy-two hours, divided into three twenty-four-hour periods, which were color coded to distinguish each. The sources of intelligence, such as agent reports or side-looking airborne radar, were designated by distinctive symbols in the proper color to denote the appropriate time period. The map was maintained continuously. This system made enemy patterns of activity more discernable, thereby facilitating timely operational decisions for the allocation of assets against enemy targets with some degree of assurance of gaining contact.

The intelligence and operational sections worked hand in glove, continuously passing information back and forth. Each brigade was assigned one or more intelligence targets daily to check out, and the allocation of the available aircraft resources was made on the basis of the overall intelligence situation. This system of assigning intelligence targets definitely increased the number of enemy contacts. The increased contacts, in turn, produced more intelligence from captured prisoners and documents, which, in turn, provided more targets. Effective targeting also ensured the most efficient utilization of combat assets, limiting the debilitating walks in the sun.

The key to utilizing intelligence was the ability to react swiftly and decisively to information. The close working relationship between the intelligence and operations sections, as well as our flexibility of operations, exemplified by the aircraft control team, allowed the division to react immediately to intelligence targets.

Improving Tactics and Techniques

By the end of 1968, the first of the division's double-barreled efforts to enhance operational capabilities had been met. That is, the maximum number of healthy, properly supported soldiers were in the field on a daily basis, night and day. Concurrent with the actions taken to maximize the paddy strengths and provide the combat soldier with aviation support and timely enemy intelligence were the division's efforts to improve combat techniques and tactics.

After the Communists' abortive attacks at Tet, the enemy retreated to his base areas to reconstitute, resupply, and plan for their next offensive, which occurred in May; then, after Mini-Tet, he literally went to ground, evading contact as much as possible. It definitely became apparent that the Viet Cong would continue his evasive actions, venturing forth only to conduct periodic highpoint attacks. The main reason for this change in tactics, from the bold attacks on Allied Forces and installations that had been conducted in the previous period, was that the Viet Cong units in our area had been defeated. The Communists were both tactically and strategically offensive oriented. To them, the defense was always a transitional phase, one used to rebuild, reorganize, and refit resources that would ultimately be used to seize the initiative. Their goal was to control as much land and population as possible.

The Communist change in tactics—long periods of evasion followed by a highpoint—required a change in the way the 9th Division operated. We had to bring the enemy to battle on our terms rather than on his. We definitely had to aggressively take the initiative to ferret him out and prevent him from reconstituting, so as to preempt his highpoint attacks.

One would think when the Viet Cong main force units withdrew to their base areas to reconstitute and refit, avoiding contact at all costs, that the enemy activities in the Delta would be quiescent. Not so: the Communists were always on the move. When the main force dispersed its units, its command and control capabilities were greatly reduced. To communicate between units, afraid that radio contacts would give away their positions, they used commo-liaison runners. Short of personnel, replacements were on the move. To refit, they required weapons and supplies which were generally delivered at night by sampans from depots in Cambodia. Afraid of being detected if they remained too long in one place, they periodically moved from one location to another. Sometimes, guerrilla forces would be required to move out and prepare main force defensive positions. Local force units were also in need of replacements, weapons, and supplies. To maintain their intimidation of the people, the local force would have to reoccupy at night the contested hamlets that the RF/PF would occupy during the day. So in our large area of responsibility, the enemy was in constant motion, especially at night. Tactics had to be developed not only to arrest their movement by attriting the enemy, thereby denying him the ability to reconstitute, but also to find the dispersed main force units and to destroy them. The first step, taken in mid-May, was to review current operations. Often, a brigade or battalion conducted a large unit operation such as a cordon and search. In a case like this, the units would be in the field for several days and then stand down for several days. During the periodic stand-downs, the enemy was not pressured. Additionally, most air operations were conducted during the day, which enabled the Viet Cong to operate at night. The solution then became obvious: the division had to operate continuously over a large area in the field both day and night, thus giving the enemy no time to reconstitute. This, then, was Major General Ewell's concept of constant pressure.

Obviously, to maintain a constant pressure, the division had to develop night tactics. With the enemy breaking down into smaller units, it was essential to operate in smaller units, day and night, to intercept the enemy's movements and to find and destroy his dispersed units. This took great courage on the part of the infantrymen.

The division developed aggressive daytime tactics that enabled it to cover a large area to dig out, surround, and destroy the dispersed Viet Cong units. It also effected unique night tactics that denied the enemy his capabilities of movement. Thus, the division improved its operational efficiency through innovative tactics suitable to the Delta terrain and the enemy's evasive posture. The constant pressure concept and the tactics and techniques evolved together, optimizing combat results with the least cost in lives and equipment, thus bringing greatly improved security to the Upper Delta, thereby accelerating pacification.

Daytime Airmobile Operations

The wide-open, inundated Delta terrain put a premium on utilizing air assets. To find and attrit a dispersed enemy, we had to adopt known tactical techniques to our special situation. Our airmobile operations required the close coordination of detailed intelligence, superbly trained air cavalry, aggressive infantry, skillful insertions, accurate artillery and tactical air firepower, and effective command and control. We called these daytime airmobile operations "jitterbugging," for reasons that will become apparent.

The requisite assets for airmobile operations were an air cavalry troop and an assault helicopter company. The assets were normally assigned to a brigade commander who, after carefully assessing all available intelligence, would select targets and, depending upon the location of the most promising opportunities, would assign the assets to one of his battalions. Coordination was effected with divisional artillery to provide fire support if necessary. If the target locations were outside the artillery fan, then arrangements were made to relocate firing batteries, often by helicopter or riverine platforms. Tactical air strikes, which could be diverted as required, were preplanned.

The air cavalry troop was the eyes (and the nose) of airmobile operations; its makeup normally consisted of the troop commander's C & C helicopter, two armed OH-6A Scout helicopters, two AH-1G Cobra gunships, and a Huey for the troop's aerial rifle platoon, which carried the airborne personnel detector (People Sniffer). Constant communications between elements was essential; the air cavalry commander controlled his units by UHF radio, monitored an FM radio on the infantry battalions net, and had one radio in the artillery net.

When the troop arrived at the designated target area, the People Sniffer helicopter would sweep the suspected area at treetop level at a speed of at least 80 knots to ensure sufficient airflow to activate the device. During the Huey sweep, the two Cobras provided cover and the two Scouts were busy reconnoitering, looking for signs of enemy movements or bunkers. Air passing through a scoop located on the underside of the helicopter was routed to the detector, where it was tested for carbon and ammonia which, in certain quantities, could indicate the potential presence of personnel. (The presence of animals such as water buffalo, however, would not give adequate readings.) We thoroughly experimented with the detector under all possible climatic conditions with varying numbers and dispersions of personnel and at different aircraft altitudes and velocities to ensure that our field utilization was optimized.[9]

We found that the utilization and effectiveness of the airborne personnel detector was influenced by many variables, such as flight patterns of the aircraft, climatology, time of day, precipitation, wind, smoke, air strikes and artillery, and the numbers and dispersion of personnel. As with everything else in the war, techniques were important. The exhaust of the aircraft affected readings, so it was important that the aircraft always be moving upwind. With inverted air temperatures, it was difficult for the scents to rise into the atmosphere, so that the maximum concentrations of the scent remained near the ground. Therefore, the aircraft should fly as low as possible above treetop level. The People Sniffer was more effective in the wet season than in the dry season because the normal temperature inversions kept the scents concentrated near the ground; in the dry season, air conducted upward reduced the concentration. The detector was not effective during precipitation, which cleansed the air of all scents. However, readings obtained following a rain definitively indicated the presence of personnel. A strong wind would transfer scent concentrations appreciable distances downwind. Our tests showed that for a twenty-five-man group, significant readings could extend for an average of three hundred meters downwind. Since smoke materially affected readings, searches were conducted upwind in areas where there was smoke. Concentrations given off by air strikes and artillery remained for at least twenty-four hours, so the operation needed to be careful to determine whether there had been recent fire support activities in the area. Our controlled tests indicated that the detector would pick up and give a maximum reading for groups of five or more personnel and that the scent buildup occurred within thirty minutes. Even if an enemy occupied a bunker or foxhole, after one hour of occupation, it would register significant readings. Although it took only thirty minutes for a significant reading to be obtained from five or more enemy, it took a minimum of three hours for the scent to decay appreciably. Since it was known that the Viet Cong moved during the night and early morning and attempted to stay hidden during the day, missions between 0900 and 1000 hrs would eliminate false recordings. However, the best opportunities for detection were thirty minutes after a rainfall. The People Sniffer was the most reliable resource in finding the dispersed enemy.

> The "Jitterbug," employed by elements of the 1st Brigade, was especially productive. The airborne personnel detector led the 3-39 Infantry into an

Fig. 9. Slicks at a landing zone

action that resulted in 30 enemy dead and several valuable prisoners. "We got some People Sniffer readings and were ready to insert when my operations officer spotted five VC and that started the whole thing," explained the Battalion Commander. Several insertions were made to block escape routes of the force estimated to be a company.

The People Sniffer was so reliable because it obtained information in real time and acted upon it immediately. Of all significant readings, 34 percent were in fact confirmed. Rarely did the Viet Cong fire at the People Sniffer aircraft, because, with the presence of the gunships and armed Scouts, retaliation was swift. The enemy soldiers generally remained hidden and bunkered down, hoping that they would not be detected. Only when inserted infantry approached their defensive positions and activated their booby trap protection would they fire.

The People Sniffer was of inestimable value in locating enemy hunkered down in inaccessible locations.

Troops faced the ever-present danger of booby traps as well as the silent Viet Cong themselves, hidden in the dense nipa palm. "If you take the most rotten and inaccessible place you can find in this country and put infantrymen there, you'll almost always find VC," said 1st Lieutenant Craig Bennett, platoon leader with the 1st Brigade. "They know Americans hate to go there with the leeches and booby traps, so they'll hide in stinking water up to their necks until we walk right up and pull them out. But that's the only way you can fight a war in the Delta."

Enemy defensive positions were often in the dense growth that lined the numerous rivers and canals with open rice paddies on either side. Such locations gave the Viet Cong clear fields of fire against oncoming infantrymen crossing the rice paddies, but they also gave us readily available landing zones. When the enemy saw that an attack was imminent he would often attempt to escape along the canals. Since these were the only avenues of escape, the enemy could be interdicted by fire and cut off by additional insertions.

When the airborne personnel detector recorded a sufficient reading, the helicopter would climb several hundred feet and eject E-58 CS canisters of tear gas. The propwash of the helicopter would spread the gas and also force it into bunkers. If Viet Cong were flushed, the aero rifle platoon could be inserted and/or the battalion commander could call for the assault helicopters to insert the infantrymen who, by fire and maneuver, would attack the target.

Initially, all insertions were made with ten slicks carrying about seventy troops. However, with the enemy breaking down into smaller units, that appeared to be ponderous, and we asked for and received permission to use five-slick insertions. Troops would be inserted three hundred meters or less from the target. If contact developed, then the second lift of five Hueys, which were on the ground standing by, were generally inserted and an attempt was made to cut off enemy escape routes.

However, if the initial target was cold, the air cavalry, attempting to locate the enemy, moved on to the next planned target, and the troops that were on the pick-up zone in reserve became the insertion force, while those on the ground reverted to the backup force. Thus, by leapfrogging the infantry units with the assault helicopters, the battalion could cover many targets in a day; this continuous action gave the name "jitterbugging" to the operation. Some units became so efficient that, should all insertions turn out to be cold, they could cover a dozen targets in a day, which was very seldom the case. Assigned targets were initially reconnoitered by pilots in a light-observation helicopter whose skill and daring were the key to locating the enemy.

> A vital ingredient in the "infantryman-helicopter team," whose teamwork was indispensable to the Division's success, is the light observation helicopter. This small craft "flies point" on "Jitterbug" operations and the alert eyes of its pilot are often the first to see the enemy. This pilot has a dangerous mission, flying very close to the ground, and valor is a way of life for him. A LOH team from D/3-5 Cavalry was reconnoitering an area when the enemy was suddenly spotted in a fortified bunker line. The lead ship was immediately enveloped by heavy ground fire and crashed. Acting quickly and with disregard for his own safety, 1Lt Hubert McMinn placed fire from his trail ship onto the enemy position in a deliberate attempt to draw fire away from the downed ship and its crew. He then landed his LOH between the crippled ship and the enemy, picked up the wounded men, and piloted his overloaded craft back to base.

If the contact appeared to be with a sizeable enemy force, then more company units became involved in an attempt to seal and pile on the enemy to prevent his escape so he could be severely attrited. Occasionally, the enemy force would be of such strength that several battalions were required to seal it, in which case the brigade commander took over the operation. Once the enemy was sealed, the heavy firepower of the artillery and tactical air was brought to bear on the "doughnut"—troops surrounding the enemy, which is the "hole"—to destroy the enemy rather than committing our infantry to frontal attacks. In that manner, our casualties were minimized. The Viet Cong usually waited until nightfall to attempt to escape the encirclement, so the troops had to keep the seal tight all night.

The Jitterbug technique was the most productive of all daytime operations because it allowed the maximum coverage of target areas and, with the air assets, facilitated the "seal-and-pile-on" tactics that were so effective. Its effectiveness was due to the aggressiveness and courage of the infantrymen and the skill of the commander involved.

Ground Mobile Operations

The highly successful airmobile operations were limited by the availability of aircraft assets, which, until January 1969, were two assault

Fig. 10. A pick-up zone

helicopter companies and two air cavalry troops, sufficient for two battalions. Consequently, almost all of our battalions were engaged in ground mobile operations. In the summer of 1968, Col. Henry E. Emerson, utilizing his earlier Vietnam experiences, adjusted previous tactics, Bushmaster and Checkerboard, to the Delta terrain and enemy situation with great success.

The Bushmaster was primarily a night operation to ambush and interdict known Viet Cong communications routes leading from heavily fortified base areas where the enemy had pretty much had a free ride. In the summer of 1968, the Viet Cong, although beaten down from the Tet and Mini-Tet Offensives, was still relatively strong. The operation initially involved an infantry company broken down into platoon elements. Its success depended greatly on good intelligence to identify the area of operations. Once the area was identified, platoon ambush sites were determined, and the company was inserted in the general area by helicopter late in the day. False insertions were often made to mislead enemy observation. After dark, the platoon moved out to its ambush sites, which had been carefully selected to be mutually sup-

Table 3. 9th Infantry Division Bushmaster operations,
27 March–26 April 1969 (units/contacts)

	Platoon	Company
Day	106/10	69/48
Night	0/0	296/91
Total	106/10	365/129

Source: Maj. Gen. Harris W. Hollis, Letter to Commanding General II Field Force, Vietnam, APO 96266, Subject: Recommendation for Award of the Presidential Unit Citation, Headquarters 9th Infantry Division, Republic of Vietnam, May 1969.

porting in case of contacts. The square area covered was generally from three-quarters of a kilometer to a full kilometer. Although the cover of darkness was important in setting up the ambush sites, the technique was also effective in the daytime, and, as the enemy was continually beaten down, daytime operations were sometimes accomplished by platoon-sized elements establishing squad-sized ambushes. From 27 March through 26 April 1969, a period when detailed records were kept, the equivalent of thirteen company days were spent on Bushmaster operations, which averaged more than four contacts per day. Note that daytime company-sized Bushmasters were very effective, making contact 70 percent of the time, while the numerous night operations had contacts 30 percent of the time.

Checkerboard tactics evolved from the Bushmaster. The Checkerboard was an offensive operation whose purpose was to find and defeat the enemy. Company units were further broken down into squad-sized elements, each of which had a fixed area of operations similar to that of a checkerboard square. Once in their assigned areas, the units would move from one terrain feature to another to interdict the enemy. The advantage of the Checkerboard was that it could cover an area twice the size of the Bushmaster. However, because of the small unit sizes, it was not suitable for areas with major enemy units. To ensure the safety of our troops, both operations were always within artillery range, and there was a light-fire helicopter team on standby. From 27 March through 26 April, the division had the equivalent of five companies in the field daily on Checkerboards. Company-sized night operations

Table 4. 9th Infantry Division Checkerboard operations, 27 March–26 April 1969 (units/contacts)

	Platoon	Company
Day	70/2	76/17
Night	0/0	61/38
Total	70/2	137/55

Source: Maj. Gen. Harris W. Hollis, Letter to Commanding General II Field Force, Vietnam, APO 96266, Subject: Recommendation for Award of the Presidential Unit Citation, Headquarters 9th Infantry Division, Republic of Vietnam, May 1969.

were the most effective, with contacts made over 60 percent of the time. Again, the key to success was the small unit leadership and the courage and aggressiveness of the soldier.

Ambushes

The 9th Division had several surveillance aids that, when utilized properly, greatly improved the division's ability to move, fight, and acquire targets at night. These included battlefield illumination, night-vision and anti-intrusion devices, and radar and aerial surveillance equipment. Of particular importance for the establishment of ambushes was the identification of enemy routes of communications. Both the radar and anti-intrusion devices were helpful in identifying patterns of enemy activity that could be used to select courses of action for the conduct of night operations. The use of starlight scopes and night observation devices provided our troops with marked improvement in visual capability over the enemy.[10]

A radar system is a means of detecting and locating targets. Our single organic AN-TPS-25 ground surveillance radar had a range of eighteen thousand meters with azimuth and range searching and tracking capabilities. It could detect a squad walking or a single man running at sixty-five hundred meters and a single man walking at three thousand meters. It provided all-weather day-and-night battlefield surveillance. The TPS-25 was augmented by several AN-PPS-5 radar sets of shorter range that could be operated by two-man teams.

The responsibility for the maintenance and operation of the divisional radar was given to the division artillery commander. These were assets of great value and were very effective in the flat Delta terrain. Recall that the Viet Cong movements to attack Saigon on 5 May were picked up by our radar, enabling the division commander to order the 5/60 Mechanized Infantry Battalion to the area where contact was made.

Seismic intrusion detectors provided a warning of movement into a specific area without the intruders being aware of detection. They were helpful in determining the use of roads and trails by the enemy, although we relied primarily upon our radar sightings.

Obviously, all areas could not be covered by surveillance devices. Much useful information was obtained from Vietnamese villagers by our Integrated Civic Action Program (ICAP). But probably the most important factor in determining the location of an ambush was the intuition of the commander.

The requirement to keep relentless pressure on the enemy night and day was primarily met by reconnaissance in force (jitterbugging) during the day and by many small unit ambushes at night operating in conjunction with Checkerboards and Bushmasters. During January, February, and March 1969, there were an average of sixty squad and platoon ambushes every night, of which 10 percent made contacts. The pressure of so many units intercepting the Viet Cong routes of communication had a disruptive effect on his operations. When our sniper program got into gear, it improved the capabilities of ambushes greatly.

A successful method used for ambushes was the stay-behind technique, whose purpose was to make the enemy believe there were no longer any Americans in the area. Sgt. Wes Watson of Company E, 75th Infantry, our Ranger group, commented on his team's sniper operation, "We inserted on choppers that were extracting an infantry company. Six armed VC came into the paddy talking and laughing. They were probably going to see if anything was left behind. They didn't know we were in the area and were caught completely unaware. Four of the six were killed outright and two left blood trails to a nearby canal where they probably drowned."[11]

Each of the battalions organized and conducted ambushes differently. The 3rd Battalion, 47th Infantry established a base camp in the middle of VC territory in Kien Hoa Province. All sources of intel-

Table 5. 9th Infantry Division Ambushes,
27 March–26 April 1969 (units/contacts)

	Squad	Platoon	Company
Day	0/0	78/11	85/129
Night	1,070/53	686/119	0/0
Total	1,070/53	764/130	85/129

Source: Maj. Gen. Harris W. Hollis, Letter to Commanding General II Field Force, Vietnam, APO 96266, Subject: Recommendation for Award of the Presidential Unit Citation, Headquarters 9th Infantry Division, Republic of Vietnam, May 1969.

ligence were exploited to include ICAP, technical devices, and input from Vietnamese district chiefs, with the objective of establishing movement patterns. The 3/47 used intrusion devices and radar to cover areas not ambushed to allow for a hasty reaction in response to sightings or activations. When the enemy was enticed into the killing zone, they sprang the ambush by detonating claymore mines, and the area was sealed with M-79 grenades and heavy direct fire. Artillery fire was also adjusted in the area of contact and along possible escape routes. The effect was devastating on the enemy.

The main VC resupply routes were the major canals in the area. Operating in the Plain of Reeds on the Bo Bo Canal one night, an ambush killed six NVA soldiers moving south in two sampans into our area. Immediately after the ambush, our infantrymen waded into the canal to recover the cargo and came up with 66 B-40 rockets, five 107 mm rockets, and an AK-47. Such constant pressure slowly strangled the enemy resupply. From 27 March to 26 April 1969, there were 1,919 ambushes, as indicated in table 5.

Snipers

The division sniper program was initiated by Major General Ewell's visit in January 1968 to the Army Marksmanship Unit at Fort Benning. The idea was to have a team from the Marksmanship Unit to train 9th Division soldiers in Vietnam in sniper tactics. Funds were made available to improve the accuracy of fifty-five M-14 rifles and to provide sniper scopes and special ammunition. The training team landed in Vietnam in June 1968, and they immediately revamped the M-16 training methods at the Reliable Academy, our training establishment for newly arrived replacements. Handpicked volunteers from each battalion attended the first class. Training was demanding, and only 50 percent of the initial class graduated, in early November 1968. The graduates were immediately reassigned to their units, and the first sniper kill was registered on 19 November. The second class graduated in early December, enabling each battalion to have six snipers and each brigade four. The hoped-for results were slow in coming, until the responsibility for sniper operations was placed on the battalion commander instead of the company commander, who really hadn't seen the potential of the program. When the battalion commander began assigning the snipers to the company going on night operations and assisting in choosing night ambush sites, the program took off. The nighttime sniper teams usually consisted of two snipers and two to four additional infantrymen for security. The use of small, highly trained teams proved successful in finding the enemy, and teams of this size were less likely to be detected. Where the sniper techniques proved successful, they were a huge boon to all nighttime ambushes. The troops gained confidence, and the results from night ambushes increased greatly. In January, February, and March 1969, there were over six thousand night ambushes, many of them accompanied by snipers. As the confidence grew, many tactical innovations were attempted.

The 6th Battalion, 31st Infantry employed night snipers from naval boats on the Mekong River with considerable success. Working in pairs, the snipers positioned themselves on the Tango boat's helicopter pad utilizing night vision devices. The boat normally traveled at a low speed, 100 to 150 meters from the shore. To assist in periods of limited illumination, they used a pink-filter xenon searchlight to extend the range of the passive vision scopes. The effect of the searchlight on the target area could not be detected by the unaided eye. Over a one-month period, the Tango boat snipers killed thirty-nine enemy at an average range of about 150 meters.

The accuracy of some snipers was phenomenal. Our most successful sniper was Sgt. Adelbert Waldron, who graduated from the division sniper school on 4 January 1969 and was assigned to the 3/60 Infantry

Table 6. 9th Infantry Division Sniper Kills, 1968–1969

December	January	February	March	April	May
11	73	93	211	346	200

Source: Quarterly Commanders' Conferences, April 1967–June 1969, 9th Infantry Division, Republic of Vietnam.

Battalion. Exhibiting outstanding bravery he operated mostly at night in a two-man group and had great success eliminating sixty-eight enemy over several months. He was awarded two Distinguished Service Crosses for his exploits. As an example, one afternoon on 24 January he was summoned to the bridge of a Tango boat because an undisclosed Viet Cong sniper was firing on the vessel from the shoreline. Sergeant Waldron, using an adjustable ranging telescope to scan the trees lining the shore, located the sniper in a palm tree. Enlisting one of the Navy watch personnel to act as his spotter, he knocked the Viet Cong sniper out of the tree with one round. The Navy duty officer reported the boat's distance from the shore at approximately seven hundred meters.[12]

Unquestionably our snipers proved to be one of the most effective tools in taking the night away from the enemy. The investment of time and effort in the sniper program, which was spearheaded by Brig. Gen. James S. Timothy, paid huge dividends. It took over a year from its inception at Fort Benning until it reached its peak performance in April 1969. Not only were the snipers themselves successful, but they raised the confidence and level of all ambush operations, enabling the division to take the night away from the Viet Cong. During January, February, and March 1969, snipers killed 377 enemy, 75 percent of which occurred during the hours of darkness, and in April 1969, their effectiveness peaked with 346 enemy killed.

The division snipers took pride in their accuracy.

> On 15 March snipers had a tremendous day. The team with 4-47 Infantry on the operation killed seven Viet Cong with seven rounds at a distance of 300 meters. As the day began, right after midnight, snipers in a night position with 3-60 Infantry had engaged and killed six enemy with six rounds, this time at a distance of 200 meters.

Fig. 11. Sgt. Adelbert Waldron takes aim

Mines and Booby Traps

A review of the operational logs indicated that mines and booby traps were a major cause of combat casualties. Every Sunday, the senior officers of the division would visit our troops in the several area hospitals, where they would see the victims of the ubiquitous Viet Cong booby traps. It was a serious issue, and like most of the division's problems, we analyzed the situation to get it under control. We gathered statistics and then published a monthly "Mine and Booby Trap Report."[13] Our goal was to alert the infantrymen on how to detect the devices and then neutralize them so as to eliminate casualties. It was Viet Cong doctrine to protect their positions with several rows of booby traps. In April 1969, the division had more than thirty-five hundred offensive operations as it aggressively and relentlessly pressured the enemy night and day. During the month, 758 mines and booby traps were encountered, of which 528, 70 percent, were neutralized. Almost all those not detonated were detected visually. The peak of booby-trap detection occurred about 1100 hrs, when the troops were fresh. On the other hand, the average peak of detonation occurred at 1600 hrs, when the troops were tired from plodding through the rice paddies up to their waists in water in the hot, humid atmosphere. Commanders were instructed to rotate units as well as lead personnel as the day progressed, so as to have as point men fresh troops who would be constantly on the alert.

It took courage to be a point man, always the first soldier to face enemy fire or to encounter a booby trap. Specialist 4 Alejandro's exploits are prime examples.

> In one of the more unusual stories of combat, Specialist 4 Jose T. Alejandro was cited for exceptional bravery on 28 February while a rifleman in Company D, 3/47 Infantry. Company D was on a reconnaissance-in-force southeast of Ben Tre when smoke grenades were thrown from helicopters flying overhead, indicating suspicious activity to the left of the company's position. Alejandro and six other infantrymen volunteered to investigate. Walking point for the tiny element, Alejandro entered a woodline and came across two Viet Cong attempting to detonate some booby traps they had planted in the area. Since the mines were obviously intended for Alejandro's companions in the rear, he charged the two enemy soldiers and engaged them in hand-to-hand combat.
>
> During the close combat with the two, Alejandro shattered the butt of his rifle. Undaunted, he took off his steel helmet and swung it like a ball and chain to ward off the enemy. Several other enemy soldiers began firing at him from a nearby bunker complex. Again, with utter disregard for his safety, Alejandro charged the bunkers, mortally wounding two of the enemy and chasing the others back into a tunnel. Having exhausted his own supply of ammunition, he picked up one of the enemy's weapons and continued toward the tunnel. Although under fire now from another location, the rifleman moved adroitly to the tunnel entrance and threw in hand grenades. When an enemy soldier who had survived the blast tried to escape the tunnel, Alejandro, still under enemy fire, stood guard at the tunnel entrance to keep him from escaping. As a result of the infantryman's gallantry, nine enemy soldiers were killed and one captured.

From April through June 1968, 17 percent of all wounded were from mines and booby traps, whereas 46 percent were from small arms fire. From January through March 1969, when the division was aggressively pressuring the enemy, only 18 percent of the troops were wounded by small arms fire, while 44 percent were wounded from mines and booby traps. In the latter period, there were over ten thousand operations, and, even though the number of booby traps detected increased from about 50 percent to 70 percent, the number of casualties from booby traps also increased.

Notwithstanding the fact that the number of booby traps detected increased to 70 percent in April, the casualties sustained that month were 16 killed and 394 wounded—41 percent and 63 percent, respectively, of all casualties.

We found that 34 percent of all booby traps were located along trails and rice paddy dikes and 36 percent were located in jungle growth; this made sense, because the enemy almost always chose his defensive positions in jungle growth and nipa trees. Seventy-two percent of all devices were grenades with tripwires attached; these could be easily neutralized by throwing a heavy object tied to a rope ahead and dragging it over the ground.

Unfortunately, 46 percent of all devices that detonated resulted in multiple casualties. This was caused by the bunching up of troops as they walked in single file, often along paddy dikes and trails. Of all booby-trap casualties, 75 percent were from multiple-casualty–producing detonations. This lack of field discipline was not acceptable. Noting the situation, we directed all commanders to take immediate and decisive action to ensure that mine and booby-trap casualties were held to a minimum.

Included in our monthly report was a handout I wrote, entitled, "The Story of a Booby Trap Casualty," which was distributed to the soldiers. It related our factual statistics to reality, and it was hoped it would help to prevent casualties. ("The Story of a Booby Trap" is included here as appendix C.)

Nighttime Airmobile Operations

Our night ground mobile operations, although effective, could only cover a limited area in our huge tactical area of operations. Once the Bushmaster, Checkerboard, and ambush units were inserted, there was little flexibility to respond to targets of opportunity elsewhere. However, our daytime airmobile operations not only covered a large area, but they had the flexibility afforded by the aircraft assets to respond to targets of opportunity. Recognizing that, our commanders started to look for ways to utilize aircraft on night operations, and several very innovative tactics were developed.

Night Hunter
Unquestionably, the Viet Cong moved primarily at night. Noting that our radars, particularly the long-range AN-TPS-25, often picked up what we thought to be sizeable enemy movements that were sometimes engaged by unobserved artillery fire, 1st Brigade Commander Col. John Geraci came up with the idea of using air cavalry to exploit the radar sightings. He and our artillery personnel worked out a plan to engage major sightings by radar-vectored air cavalry—simple in concept but extremely complex in execution. The technique worked like this: whenever the AN-TPS-25 found a movement of twenty or more personnel, they would carefully monitor the sighting to be sure that it was as best they could determine an enemy group. They then alerted artillery and the air cavalry. Given the coordinates, the artillery battery prepared to fire a volley of high-explosive rounds on the target as well as two illuminating rounds to guide the air cavalry to the target. The air cavalry commander vectored his two Cobra gunships toward the sighting on a flight path perpendicular to the artillery-gun target line and at an altitude lower than the agreed-upon height of burst of the illuminating rounds. With proper timing, the gunships would be able to exploit the explosive effect of the artillery. If the sighting happened to be near a populated area, then only the illuminating rounds were fired, with the gunships attacking the target. In the event of a very large sighting, a ground element could be alerted.

The division was always interested in innovative tactics and gave Colonel Geraci the go-ahead in early December 1968. The first Night Hunter was a success, killing twenty enemy. It was successfully attempted several more times, but the shortcomings of the technique didn't make it feasible for the long haul. First, it was tied to the location of the AN-TPS-25 and could not interdict areas beyond artillery range. More important, the area coverage was limited. Then, the air cavalry was on stand-by, and there were many nights without a major sighting. Additionally, it was an extremely complex technique, requiring excellent coordination and split-second timing. Notwithstanding,

Enhancing Combat Capabilities 73

Fig. 12. A soldier on a rice-paddy dike

the Night Hunter operation conclusively proved that air cavalry could operate effectively at night, and it led to the very successful night search technique.

Night Search
The night search was basically an air cavalry operation normally requiring only a command and control helicopter with a few infantrymen and two Cobras. Initially, operational areas were selected based on known enemy movement patterns and current intelligence. Later, with so very many canals and rivers in the area, random search patterns were organized covering large areas, giving the division at least the broad coverage we enjoyed with the daytime airmobile operations. The enemy's movement at night was therefore drastically curtailed.

The Night Search operation was led by the command and control aircraft containing spotters flying about four hundred feet over the target area. In the beginning, the spotters used Starlight scopes to search the trails and canals below for enemy movement. When they identified a target, they fired a burst of tracer rounds to mark it, and the Cobras flying at about fifteen hundred feet zoomed in for the kill. Starting in January 1969, when they became available, many battalions used snipers as "spotters," and their accurate fire eliminated many enemy. Constant viewing through a sniper scope was visually extremely tiring and we then began using the larger night observation device to identify targets. By trial and error, techniques greatly improved.

The spotters' primary purpose was to locate otherwise unseen enemy on the ground. It took concentration and training for the snipers to scan from the moving aircraft and learn to account for the effects of aircraft movement when marking and engaging targets. Best results were obtained between 2000 and 2400 hrs, when enemy movement was at its peak. However, it didn't take long for the Viet Cong to adjust to our operational patterns, and we had to adjust our times of operation.

When ambient light conditions were insufficient to activate the night vision devices, artificial illumination was delivered by either artillery or another helicopter. To not alert the enemy in the area being searched, the illumination was offset by several kilometers. We found that the VC under the illumination remained hidden while those in the area of search relaxed, thinking the action was elsewhere, and we were able to have great results. Some units took to having offset illumination during good lighting conditions to lull the Viet Cong into complacency.

The night search operations enabled the division to cover large swaths of territory, severely limiting enemy night movements.

> An extended Night Search by ships from the 9th Aviation Battalion and men from 2/39 Infantry was extraordinarily successful. Some facts about this search help explain the effectiveness of the techniques. The search lasted about six and one half hours, the first kill coming at 2025 hrs on 25 April. During this period of time, the spotters in the command and control helicopter, who both mark the target with tracer fire and provide target surveillance, counted fifty-two enemy bodies. These Viet Cong were killed at nineteen separate locations in groups of one to six. The search covered virtually the whole of Base Area 470 in western Dinh Tuong, an area of concentrated Viet Cong activity which lies astride a major route of infiltration into the Delta. Flying low along the wooded streams and canals, the spotters detected two sure signs of the enemy through their Starlight scopes, moving sampans and campfires. These convincing signs

Table 7. 9th Infantry Division Night Search Operations, 1969

	January	February	March	April	May
Total operations	19	37	60	43	60
Total VC killed	134	373	477	388	300
Killed per operation	7.0	10.1	7.9	9.0	5.0

Source: Quarterly Commanders' Conferences, April 1967–June 1969, 9th Infantry Division, Republic of Vietnam.

of Viet Cong presence were corroborated in some instances by ground fire. Brave pilots and marksmen are required to execute the Night Search mission and the tremendous success of this tactic testifies to their capabilities.

Again, the enemy was in constant motion, resupplying, reinforcing, relocating, and moving to attack positions, almost always at night. The night search operations enabled the division to cover a large area at night, complementing the daytime Jitterbug operations, thereby enabling the division to keep constant pressure on the Viet Cong. Not only was the Night Search effective in exterminating the enemy, but the tactic was essentially casualty-free. As Night Search techniques improved and the tactic, which originated with the 1st Brigade, was adopted by the other two brigades, the success of operations continued to increase, peaking in March (see table 7). Ultimately, Night Search tactics spread to other divisions in Vietnam, where excellent tactical results were also obtained.

When I briefed the South Vietnamese Joint Staff on night search techniques, my good friend Colonel Tho, the JGS J-3, visited the division in late December to go on an operation. Upon his return to Dong Tam, he was elated and said that he could easily spot the VC and that the operation had killed eighteen enemy.

Night Raid

The most daring of all the division's tactical innovations was the Night Raid. It was formulated by Capt. Joseph Hudson, the intelligence officer of the 2nd Battalion, 39th Infantry. Intelligence information obtained from villagers on our Integrated Civic Action Programs, as well as from Hoi Chanhs, indicated that although guerrillas and local force companies dispersed during the daytime, they congregated back together in the VC-controlled hamlets and isolated houses at night. Captain Hudson suggested if that was the only time the local VC concentrated, then let's go after them. Thus, the concept of the night raid was formulated. The operation as finally conceived consisted of a command and control helicopter, two Cobras, and two Hueys, carrying five to seven infantrymen each. The plan was to pick a hamlet or other location based upon the latest intelligence. The troops were thoroughly briefed as to the layout of the area and what they expected to find. At a prearranged time, the artillery would fire illuminating rounds, the command and control (C&C) helicopter would mark the LZ, and the two slicks protected by the Cobras would insert the troops and then lift off and circle the area waiting to extract. The element of surprise was critical in this daring attack. The raid rarely lasted more than five minutes. When the enemy had been eliminated or prisoners had been captured, the Hueys landed, picked up the team, and departed rapidly. The gunships provided the extra firepower needed to isolate the area and to support the ground force.

We thought long and hard before authorizing a Night Raid. We scrubbed the technique thoroughly, making certain that all the combatants knew the procedures. There was a chance that we could lose two helicopters and a dozen of our finest infantrymen. I finally gave permission in March, and Captain Hudson led the initial raid. It was very successful, and several more followed. Most of them were done by the 2nd Battalion, 39th Infantry and by our Rangers. In all, they killed a substantial number and took a dozen prisoners, who were often captured when sound asleep, without the loss of a single helicopter but with the loss of two brave infantrymen. One of the Rangers' most successful raids resulted in thirteen enemy dead. According to Sgt. Michael Glawinski, "One enemy was killed as he gathered up a pile of AK-47 rifles. They were so surprised when we opened up that some of them were still sitting at tables."

The Night Raids were a severe psychological shock to the Viet Cong when they realized that they were no longer safe at night in their hamlets and hooches:

> Company E, 2-39 Infantry, executed a Night Raid on an intelligence target west of Cai Be and killed fifteen enemy. As artillery illumination

lit the target area, 9th Aviation Battalion helicopters touched down and the infantrymen quickly diffused into the area. The enemy was taken by complete surprise. "The minute our presence was known, the whole area was crawling with people," said Major John Purdy, Battalion Operations Officer. "Most of them were running like crazy for the woodline." Ninth Aviation gunships killed seven Viet Cong in the woodline and the infantrymen killed eight.

Or, as another example: In Dinh Tuong, on 11 March, the 9th Aviation Battalion displayed its flexibility as its helicopters assumed the dual role of air cavalry and assault support. Helicopter gunners downed ten Viet Cong during a Night Raid in the early morning hours and killed another twelve on a Night Search shortly before midnight. A participant in the Night Raid, 1st Lt Robert Walker, commented on the success of this tactic, "They just don't expect to be hit at such a late hour. It's unheard of to have a batch of crazy GIs running around killing VC at 4:00 a.m."

The nighttime airmobile operations did not require many infantry assets but were totally dependent upon the availability of the air cavalry and some assault helicopters. The great improvement in aircraft maintenance allowed the utilization of the air cavalry at night. However, it further burdened the wonderful maintenance personnel, whose responsibility was to keep the aircraft operationally ready. One cannot praise enough the intrepid pilots, whose flying prowess was nothing short of fantastic, and the brave soldiers who participated. The Night Search and the daytime Jitterbug operations enabled large portions of our operating area to be covered, keeping a constant pressure on the enemy night and day.

It took great courage to operate at night, particularly when inserting troops on the ground.

> Airmobile operations at night are particularly hazardous. Coordination and control of the helicopters and ground troops, if an insertion takes place, is especially difficult. Aggressiveness and individual courage are essential if such tactics are to be successful and not involve large friendly casualties. An important reason the 9th Division infantrymen demonstrated these qualities so consistently was their fearless leadership. The actions of Capt. William Perkins during the Night Search by the 3/60 Infantry illustrate this. His small force encountered only very light contact after an insertion, and a slick was called in to pick up the group. The ship received a

sudden burst of heavy fire as it touched down, and in the rush to complete the pick-up it left one man on the ground. Captain Perkins directed the pilot to land again in the dark. During the descent, he was wounded in the leg and hand, and though he struggled to control the ship, it crashed, pinning him beneath it. Freed from the wreckage and painfully wounded, the captain directed the firefight and controlled the extraction of every member of his force. He departed the area on the last chopper.

At the end of December 1968, daytime offensive operations, particularly the Jitterbug, had been doing very well. The number and effectiveness of the Bushmaster, Checkerboard, and ambush night operations had been increasing, and with the implementation of the Night Search and the improvement in sniper activities, it was felt that the second of the division's objectives to improve combat operations, that is, to develop the techniques and tactics necessary to make the infantryman in the field effective in applying constant pressure on the enemy, had been met.

Chapter 4

Pacification: The Endgame

The 9th Infantry Division was introduced in the Delta for one purpose only, to improve the security. Its mission was clear: it had to defeat the Viet Cong main and local force units and to support the pacification efforts of the GVN, thereby eliminating the Viet Cong's intimidation of the people. Pacification then was the endgame, and the most discernable pattern in it was that programs depended entirely upon security. Consequently, the division had a dual focus—combat operations and pacification.

A Guerrilla War

In mid-1968, the war in the populated Delta of South Vietnam was a guerrilla war. The tactics of avoiding contact only to surface at high points and then to disappear into the countryside and the absolute necessity of the Viet Cong main and local force units to have the support of the people to operate effectively were hallmarks of guerrilla warfare. In this guerrilla war, the goals of both the Communists and the GVN and its allies was to control the population and resources of South Vietnam. Since the GVN controlled the urban areas, the pacification of the rural areas was the key to success. Although many peasants harbored ill feelings toward the government for past deprivations, it was generally necessary for the Communists to maintain control of the countryside through force and intimidation. Their main and local force battalions provided the muscle, and the local district companies and village and hamlet guerrillas kept the lid on popular discontent. The Viet Cong manipulated the population by imposing its own Infrastructure (VCI). The VC coerced people into providing food, intelligence, and labor and, most importantly, unit recruits. The hamlet guerrillas dug the bunkers, emplaced the booby traps, transported materiel, and provided localized intelligence. Control of the rural population was the Communists' number-one objective. To wrest control from the Communists and provide security to the countryside, the Allies not only had to defeat the Viet Cong main and local force units, but they had to block the increased infiltration of NVA troops, supplies, and equipment that were bolstering the failing efforts of the Viet Cong, as well as eliminate the important VCI. That required the full cooperation of all Allied Forces and GVN organizations.

Between 1965 and 1971, the Communists were fighting a guerrilla war. However, it is important to note that, over time, they set aside all pretense that the conflict was an indigenous insurrection, abandoning guerrilla warfare and adopting conventional warfare methods. These conventional tactics accelerated as the United States withdrew its 500,000-man force, leaving the 290,000 NVA/VC troops in place. These enemy troops were upgraded with tanks, heavy artillery, and anti-aircraft guns. NVA tactics improved to the point that they were making coordinated divisional-sized combined arms attacks upon the thinly stretched and always outnumbered RVNAF units. Although the NVA changed its tactics, the GVN stubbornly clung to its strategy of pacifying and protecting all twelve thousand far-flung hamlets and villages. Even after the United States drastically reduced its military aid funding in 1974, which forced the RVNAF to conserve ammunition and greatly reduce VNAF flying hours, thereby appreciably limiting the previous RVNAF advantages of firepower and mobility, the GVN did not adjust to the situation. The RVNAF, attempting to protect all the population and territory, was stretched too thin without adequate reserves. A major factor causing the NVA/VC to change their tactics was that the GVN and its allies were very successful in their pacification efforts.[1]

The Tug of War

There was a great tug of war between the Communists and the GVN to control the rural population. Earlier, the GVN did not have sufficient forces to protect the thousands of hamlets and villages. Often, RVNAF units would visit hamlets during the day; however, at night, when they left, the VC would occupy them. It didn't take much for the VC with guns to intimidate the peace-loving farmers.

However, by mid-1968, the GVN was poised to expand its security out from the urban areas and to reclaim the countryside. The tools for providing security had improved immeasurably. The Ministry of Revolutionary Development had been formed to coordinate the activities of the many military and civilian organizations involved in pacification. The Regular Forces (ARVN) were conducting operations directly in support of pacification. The RF/PF had expanded and were better equipped and led. The People's Self Defense Force had been formed and was increasing greatly, and was assisting the RF/PF in local security. The Phoenix Program implemented by the National Police had been initiated for the purpose of identifying and rooting out the VCI personnel. The police utilized provincial reconnaissance units, made up of Chieu Hoi personnel as a strike force in eliminating VCI. Working together with the Popular Forces, the National Police maintained law and order in the villages and hamlets. Once secure, the rural development cadres moved in to improve the social and economic well-being of the population. With those building blocks in place and the Viet Cong main forces in their base areas, from 1 November 1968 to 31 January 1969, the GVN carried out the Accelerated Pacification Campaign, whose purpose it was to expand the control of the GVN.

The life of a peasant in peacetime was difficult enough. The war, with its added deprivations, made the situation even more difficult. The farmers were tied to the land and could not vote with their feet, as hundreds of thousands of other South Vietnamese had done when they moved to GVN-controlled areas. Although poor, the farmers were wise; they would not willingly commit themselves to either side unless there was a solid sense of security. As a result, many hamlets remained contested as the Communists and the GVN fought for control. The control of the Delta countryside was paramount to the GVN in this period of guerrilla warfare, since it would take away from the Communists their source of sustenance and manpower and deny them the bases from which to attack urban areas.

The Hamlet Evaluation System

One may ask, how do you measure or define control? MACV went to great pains to answer that fundamental question.[2] It designed the Hamlet Evaluation System (HES) specifically as a means of assessing the effects of insurgency upon the people of Vietnam. Essentially, it permitted a set of questions to be asked about the people and their environment and evaluations to be derived from the responses. The system provided information in three fundamental areas encompassing pacification—military, political, and community development—from a set of 165 multiple-choice questions. HES data originated at the hamlet and village level with information gathered monthly from various sources. It was designed to meet several objectives, the most important of which were to monitor the progress of the pacification effort in hamlets and villages throughout South Vietnam and to provide a geopolitical profile of South Vietnam.

The general types of inputs to the system are shown in figure 13. The output was a rating for each hamlet/village in country. There were seven basic alphabetic ratings forming a progressive scale, from worst to best. An "E" rating represented the worst situation; an "A" represented the best; and "D," "C," and "B" ratings marked intermediate levels. An "N" was assigned if there was insufficient information to evaluate a hamlet and a "V" was given when the hamlet was considered under VC control.

In 1968–1969, the security ratings were based primarily upon the military situation, but in later years, the security rating was determined by combining the military and political situations. A "V" rating was given if enemy forces physically occupied the hamlet. An "A" rating could be assigned if there was no enemy military activity during the month, or if governmental units occupied the hamlet. A hamlet was considered to be under GVN control if it had a HES rating of "A" or "B" and under Communist control if it had a "V" rating. Control was contested when the ratings were "C," "D," and "E," although a hamlet with a "C" was considered under the influence of the GVN and a hamlet with a "D" or "E" was considered under the influence of the VC.

Actually, the control of the population in the Upper Delta had not changed appreciably during 1967, and the control situation just before the Tet Offensive on 30 January 1968 is as shown below. For comparative purposes, the control situation on 31 May 1968, following the Tet and Mini-Tet Offensives is also indicated. On 31 January 1968 only 92,952 inhabitants out of 1,715,948 were living in an "A" rated hamlet, and there was not a single "A" rated hamlet in either Go Cong or Long An provinces.

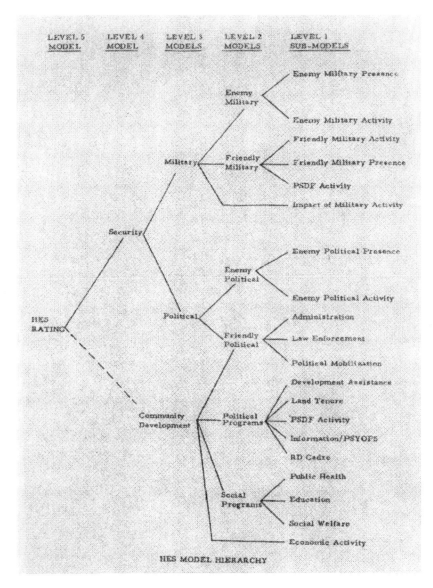

Fig. 13. Hamlet Evaluation System model hierarchy

Table 8. The Hamlet Control Situation

Province	Total population*	GVN control (A, B)	VC control (V)	Contested (C, D, E)
Dinh Tuong	588,381	151,804	230,642	183,942
Kien Hoa	570,190	74,953	258,830	236,410
Go Cong	168,917	49,569	40,210	76,138
Long An	388,460	33,515	132,268	133,307
Total 31 January 1968	1,715,948	309,841	661,950	629,797
Total 31 May 1968	1,721,317	285,101	653,660	662,217

Source: Hamlet Evaluation Survey, 31 January 1968 and 31 May 1968.
Note: *About 115,000 people lived in non-hamlet areas.

The two phases of the Communist General Offensive and General Uprising were unsuccessful in bringing the population under VC control. There had been no general uprising in this key populated Delta area. In fact, there was a decrease in the population under VC control. Early in 1968 was the apogee of VC control in the Upper Delta (including the period prior to the 1975 collapse of the GVN). In May 1968, only 16.6 percent of the population was under GVN control, whereas 38.7 percent was under Communist control. Over 660,000 inhabitants lived in contested hamlets. The security and pacification operations of the 9th Division and its RVNAF allies were to dramatically improve the situation in the coming months.

Invading VC Base Areas

About June 1968, the division took a bold step and directed the 1st Brigade to establish a battalion-sized fire support base (FSB) in the heart of VC territory near Base Area 470. Plans were carefully made to insert troops, establish a perimeter, and then quickly fortify the perimeter to withstand expected enemy attacks. Everything went smoothly. The VC were obviously caught by surprise and offered only small resistance. The FSB was expanded and built up, an oasis in the previously sacrosanct VC territory from which the enemy could more easily be attacked and

Table 9. Hamlet Evaluation Ratings, Kien Hoa, 31 May 1968

Ratings	Hamlet		Population	
	Number	Percentage	Number	Percentage
A	4	0.7	8,226	1.4
B	30	4.9	39,893	7.0
C	143	23.3	186,483	32.6
D	76	12.4	77,685	13.6
E	7	1.1	3,525	0.6
V	347	56.6	255,712	44.7
Abandoned	6	0.1	–	–
Total	613	100	571,524	100

Source: Hamlet Evaluation Survey, Kien Hoa, 31 May 1968.

interdicted. Subsequently, other FSBs were constructed in VC areas. In July, when the 2nd Brigade established an FSB in Kien Hoa, the VC responded viciously with mortar fire and ground attacks, however, to no avail. Units operating from these FSBs, utilizing ambushes as well as Bushmaster and jitterbug techniques, took the battle right into the center of VC territory, seriously attriting the VC and disrupting efforts to resupply and refit. The VC hegemony over the Delta countryside was broken. GVN pacification results began to increase at this time, surging in early 1969 during the IV Corps Dry Weather Campaign.

As a matter of interest, 31 May 1968 HES ratings for Kien Hoa, the province where VC control was greatest, are given in table 9. As mentioned, prior to the establishment of a battalion fire support base in Kien Hoa in July 1968, there were ten times as many hamlets controlled by the VC than by the GVN. Kien Hoa, a bastion of VC hegemony, was a prime area for security and pacification operations.

The Pacification Process

Pacification was a complex process requiring the coordination and cooperation of Allied military forces and GVN civilian ministries. In accordance with the HES model, it entailed three distinct stages:

1. (Military) *Establish Security:* This was generally accomplished by either U.S. or ARVN units driving off the VC main and local force units.
2. (Political) *Stabilize the Situation:* This occurred when RF, PF, PSDF, and National Police units were able to purge the hamlets of VC guerrillas and infrastructure and GVN cadres were able to operate and establish political institutions.
3. (Community Development) *Enhance Development:* This included provisions of health and educational facilities, initiation of social welfare programs, establishment of land tenure, et cetera.

The first two steps in the pacification process could just as well apply to Communist efforts to gain control by driving off Allied military units and stabilizing the situation with local forces and guerrillas, allowing the VCI to establish a political apparatus. Control was not an irreversible process—the contest could go either way. That's what tug of war was all about.

Integrating Combat Operations

The 9th Infantry Division utilized the HES extensively to integrate our combat operations with our pacification efforts to ensure the optimum support for the pacification program. When the Accelerated Pacification Campaign was initiated in late 1968, it had clear-cut objectives; the most fundamental one was to choose key hamlets and villages that were in a contested status with the Viet Cong and, through security and civic efforts, to raise these hamlets to a more secure GVN status. We had little faith in the HES initially, since it appeared to us that it could be a pencil exercise with little validity. Therefore, we undertook a detailed Hamlet Evaluation Survey for all the hamlets in one district of Dinh Tuong Province. We told our G-2 to be hardnosed in his evaluations. At the conclusion of our survey, we compared it with the MACV, Advisory Team Survey. We were literally amazed to find that there was less than a 10% difference in evaluations. This gave us new and substantial confidence in the HES. Consequently, the Division integrated combat and pacification efforts in support of the Accelerated Pacification Campaign. We utilized the monthly HES classifications to assess the progress of pacification in our area, increasing our efforts in the vicinity of the contested and VC-controlled hamlets. The Division continually coordinated combat operations with Civic Action, and these integrated efforts materially assisted the GVN pacification program.

The 9th Division pacification program had five major Civic Action themes: 1) psychological operations to win the hearts and minds of the people, 2) assistance to victims of the war, 3) assistance in health matters, 4) educational assistance, and 5) the repair and construction of facilities. The individual American soldier has always generously helped to alleviate the suffering and anguish caused by wars, and Vietnam was no exception.[3]

All units of the division participated diligently and generously in civic action and psychological activities to advance the course of pacification. In the January through May 1969 period, there were 5,357 medical team visits; more than half were to contested hamlets, which treated 344,336 patients. Over 3,800 hours of loudspeaker PSYOP missions were conducted, and 87,714,000 leaflets were distributed, mostly by airdrop. Food and clothing were distributed, thirty schools were repaired or constructed, and 9,302 school kits given out. To improve local transportation, 164 kilometers of roads and 124 bridges were repaired or constructed. Vigorous efforts by the soldiers, often from their own means, were made to improve the health, education, and well-being of the inhabitants.[4]

We brought one of our finest combat soldiers, Maj. Bernard Loeffke, in to Division Headquarters to be the G5 supervising civic actions in both friendly and enemy psychological operations. With respect to enemy-oriented PSYOPS, the G5 orchestrated well-planned actions to induce enemy troops to rally to the GVN cause. Millions of leaflets were air dropped with varying messages. Whenever there was a major contact, loudspeakers were employed to lower the enemy's morale and to induce NVA/VC to surrender. Such actions were highly successful in the division area; 8,949 Viet Cong cadres surrendered. It was axiomatic that the greater our military pressure on the enemy, the greater the number of ralliers. Often the enemy would rally to the RNVAF units in our area because of language compatibility.

Little has been mentioned concerning the VC propaganda efforts directed toward U.S. forces. Notwithstanding, they continuously distributed leaflets to American troops, and they often displayed large

Fig. 14. Viet Cong propaganda leaflet

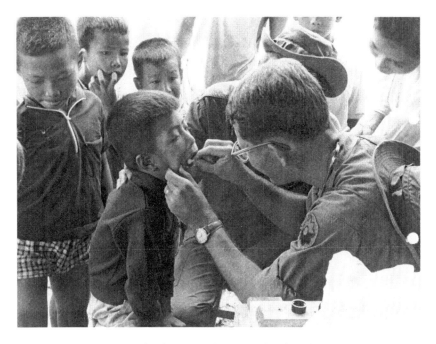

Fig. 15. MEDCAP—medical personnel treating local civilians

propaganda banners in the smaller hamlets. Their most popular themes were directed towards family separations, particularly at holidays, and the fear of becoming a casualty. Initial VC propaganda efforts were quite clumsy but they became more sophisticated over time. Figure 14 shows the front and back of a typical VC leaflet, which plays upon both holiday anxieties and the fear of being wounded. Interestingly, the most effective U.S. enemy psychological action was a record which was broadcast from a helicopter flying over an enemy area at night which had as its theme a baby crying to see its NVA/VC absent father.

Our most effective civic action was the Medical Civic Action Program (MEDCAP). Almost every day teams composed of medical personnel accompanied by infantrymen for protection traveled throughout the friendly areas of the provinces visiting hamlets to provide medical treatment to Vietnamese civilians. In a one-year span, over 500,000 patients were treated. Our MEDCAPs were so well appreciated by the populace that we decided to send the teams into contested hamlets to integrate civic action and PSYOP efforts with intelligence gathering activities. We always cleared our visits with the local District Chiefs and usually our teams were accompanied by Regional or Popular Forces. We called this innovation our Integrated Civic Action Program (ICAP), whose purpose was to collect information on the enemy while providing humanitarian assistance and attempting to improve GVN acceptance in local hamlets/villages. ICAPs were our most successful source of human intelligence. And we prepared a pamphlet for distribution detailing the conduct of an ICAP.[5]

During the day, the hamlets were normally almost devoid of men folk since they were either in the military or working in the fields. ICAPs, obviously, were generally conducted by male personnel; and the Vietnamese women, even if there was no language barrier, would not talk to the soldiers. So at first it was difficult to obtain intelligence information, although the villagers on hand were medically treated. We hit upon the idea of hiring women Hoi Chanhs who had rallied as female Tiger Scouts. They then conversed with the women villagers and often obtained a wealth of information concerning VC activities.

As stated, contested hamlets were often controlled by the GVN during the day but when government personnel withdrew in the evening, they were subject to Viet Cong pressure and occupation at night. Therefore, our ICAPs on many occasions would spend the evening in the hamlets to ensure security, and we called these actions NITECAPs. In the period January through April 1969, the Division conducted 2,042 MEDCAPs, 2,754 ICAPs, and 561 NITECAPs, 45 per day, which treated 344,336 Vietnamese.

The Division fully supported the GVN's pacification program. It was obvious that for pacification to succeed in our area, it had to be accomplished with the full cooperation of the RVNAF and also GVN entities.

A Cooperative Effort with the RVNAF

The 9th Division benefitted greatly in our operations and in our pacification efforts from the spirit of cooperation that existed between it and the RVNAF, which included the 7th ARVN Division in Dinh Tuong, Kien Hoa, and Go Cong Provinces and the 25th ARVN Division in Long An Province, as well as many RF companies and PF platoons.

Operations were planned and conducted, and tactical information and intelligence were continuously exchanged at all levels of command to ensure timely and coordinated efforts.

In September 1968, while in command of the 1st Brigade, I was asked to make an evaluation of the ARVN and RF units located in Long An Province, which at the time were six ARVN battalions, three each from the 46th and 50th Infantry Regiments of the 25th ARVN Division, and twenty-five RF companies.[6] An additional three RF companies were in training and another three had been authorized but not yet organized. There was a large disparity in the geographical distribution of units: for example, ARVN battalions were located in only two of the seven districts, and the Thu Thua District, with a population of forty-three thousand, had only two RF companies, whereas the smaller Rach Kien District, with eighteen thousand inhabitants, had three RF companies. Any major improvement in spoiling and preemptive offensive operations as well as security would require restationing ARVN units and redistributing RF companies, particularly with the six authorized but not assigned units. Neither of the ARVN regiments was highly aggressive. Both were terrain-oriented, and their operations were characterized by sweeps that picked at the enemy. Their use of air assets was marginal in that they did not strike with them but utilized them for transportation to a location where a stilted operation had been planned. It was noted, however, that when on a joint operation, the ARVN did move out well, indicating a pride of unit and perhaps increased confidence. The 1st Brigade had conducted three joint operations recently. The RF companies in Long An fighting at home were highly motivated and very familiar with the terrain and, as a result, often performed comparably to the ARVN. In the most recent U.S. Advisors Territorial Evaluation of Forces in Long An Province—in which they rated for responsiveness to orders, weapons proficiency, leadership and unit esprit, and plans for supportive fire—thirteen of the RF companies were rated as "good" and twelve as "satisfactory." In summary, I believed at the time that the ARVN and RF/PF picture was good. There was room for improvement, and there was a general willingness on their part to improve. The best vehicle to obtain a general upgrading was by increased U.S.-VN joint participation in operations. This evaluation of RVNAF units probably applied as well to those in

IV Corps. The RF/PF units were those that were constantly in the countryside providing the safety of "secure" hamlets and assisting in rooting out the enemy in "contested" hamlets, particularly the Viet Cong Infrastructure.

Later in December 1968, General Ewell established an evaluation program for RVNAF units in the division's area. We began keeping statistical data on the Vietnamese units, which was provided by their U.S. advisors with the goal of having them increase their combat operations and, through analysis, their operational effectiveness. Through our war experiences, we knew that small increases in the number and effectiveness of operations could lead to large increases in the number of enemy eliminated. To further joint efforts, the 9th Infantry Division commander sponsored a weekly conference of key U.S. and Vietnamese personnel from each province, at which the statistical data was reviewed and ideas exchanged. In that manner, lessons learned and effective combat techniques were systematically exchanged.

The 9th Division took steps to improve RVNAF operations by conducting a six-week program of basic unit training for the 25th ARVN Division and training in air cavalry and airmobile techniques for the 7th ARVN Division. Sniper training was given to cadres from the Central Training Command, seven ARVN divisions, the airborne division, and the Ranger command. To evaluate the effectiveness of training, our instructors accompanied units of the 25th ARVN Division on combat operations, on which several of our troops were wounded.

General Ewell gave considerable thought to upgrading ARVN and RF/PF forces in our TAOI. A formula was developed that we thought would work; it stated that the operational effectiveness of a unit, defined as the enemy eliminated per company day of troops available, was equal to the utilization of these troops times the efficiency of these troops. It defined utilization as the company days spent in the field divided by the company days available and efficiency as the number of enemy eliminated per company day in the field. Thus, utilization and efficiency are entirely different matters, both of which contributed to operational effectiveness.[7]

The approach was first to get the RVNAF forces out of their compounds and into the field, that is, to improve their utilization. In this, we were quite successful. Before we started, RVNAF forces in our

Table 10. Operational Effectiveness, Recommended Goals, 9 May 1968

		South Vietnamese popular and regional forces	Army of the Republic of Vietnam	U.S. Forces
Utilization	Company day in the field per company day available	0.50	0.50	0.75
Efficiency	Enemy eliminated per company day in the field	0.30	0.75	1.50
Operational effectiveness	Enemy eliminated per company day available	0.15	0.38	1.13

Source: Maj. Gen. Harris W. Hollis, Letter to Lt. Col. William B. Rosson (Operational Effectiveness), 9 May 1968. Headquarters 9th Infantry Division, Republic of Vietnam.

TAOI went to the field an average of once every three days. They then began operating every other day, which was the standard we set. The U.S. standard was that our troops should be operational three days out of four, but because of the prolonged combat the RVNAF faced and because they generally had their families with them, we considered a 50 percent utilization as most satisfactory.

The second step in our attempt to increase the operational effectiveness was to improve RVNAF efficiency, that is, once operating in the field to show them how to eliminate more VC. In that respect, we had some, but not great, success. ARVN forces still continued to sweep in battalion-sized operations, and they seldom operated at night. The RF/PF, although they operated about 50 percent of the time in company-sized units as well as at night, did not have adequate training in such areas as basic marksmanship, nor did they have the leadership as yet to operate efficiently during the period of RF/PF expansion when leadership skills were stretched.

The ARVN units did begin to operate a little more at night and attempted to learn airmobile and jitterbug tactics when they had aviation assets so that there was a gradual but steady improvement. The

Fig. 16. ARVN soldiers

recommended goals established for operational effectiveness in the 9th Division TAOI, if successfully attained, would result in thirty-six hundred enemy eliminated per month (see table 10). The timely exchange of information and intelligence and the coordinated and cooperative efforts between the RVNAF and the 9th Infantry Division contributed greatly to mutual success and the advancement of the pacification program.

An example of the exchange of intelligence by Regional Forces and the rapid exploitation of the information occurred in Long An on 23 April 1969; this involved a platoon of B/2-47 Mechanized Infantry:

> Late in the evening of 23 April the platoon received information from a Regional Forces outpost that an unknown number of Viet Cong were concealed in a woodline northwest of their outpost (XS 480685). The mechanized platoon deployed and moved into the area where ten to fifteen Viet Cong were observed and engaged with organic weapons. Artillery fires were called in to fix the enemy in position and gunships from B/3-

17 Cavalry interdicted possible avenues of escape. "Spooky," an Air Force flareship armed with miniguns, provided illumination and more firepower. The enemy's fire was silenced shortly after midnight, but illumination and friendly fire continued throughout the night. A sweep of the area established that twenty enemy had been killed by the infantry, artillery, and miniguns. Several weapons were captured and destroyed. Two U.S. soldiers were wounded.

Infiltration

Prior to 1968, the Viet Cong had had little difficulty in recruiting the intimidated and often disenchanted rural population to fill their units. The North Vietnamese had carefully insisted that COSVN units be composed of only South Vietnamese, so they could report that the insurrection in SVN was strictly a South Vietnamese affair. However, after the huge VC personnel losses in phases 1 and 2 of the General Offensive and General Uprising, the North Vietnamese gave up on this subterfuge and began to infiltrate NVA troops into the Delta to supplant VC losses and units.

The military materiel required to support the Viet Cong insurgency in the Delta had always been brought from sources in North Vietnam. At this time, supplies for the Delta region were generally offloaded at the Cambodian port of Sihanoukville and stored at NVA storage sites near the Cambodian border. As the result of large equipment losses, to resupply the depleted Viet Cong units there was a steady flow of weapons and ammunition into the Upper Delta. Since movement was easily observed in the open Delta areas, NVA troops and materiel were normally infiltrated at night by sampan on the myriad of waterways in the region. Therefore, to prevent the Viet Cong from reconstituting his forces, it was important to interdict enemy personnel and supplies. The Night Search was a valuable tactic, enabling the division to range far and wide interdicting the waterways at night. But so were the ambush and jitterbug operations. The division focused on the enemy, attacking as he attempted to transport materiel, and, once it located Viet Cong storage sites, the division would revisit the area to ambush the enemy as they attempted to resupply. The incidents related here are a few examples of the successful interdiction of troops, weapons, and supplies.

On 8 April, southeast of the town of Ben Luc in Long An Province, a company from 2-47 Infantry established night ambush positions near the location of a substantial weapons cache which had been discovered in late March. An enemy force, estimated to consist of seventy-five men, returned to the area, apparently to resupply, and in a two-hour period beginning at 2050 hrs, A/2-47 Infantry killed 42 and captured one. The enemy force was identified as part of the North Vietnamese Army K4 Battalion. A platoon sergeant, whose ambush patrol was within 200 meters of the cache site, described the detection of the NVA force: "They moved right by our position, some as close as five meters. We let them pass before opening up. They had begun to poke around where the cache had been hidden." Another sergeant commented that the enemy force had been well-disciplined and maintained, but the surprise and ferocity of the ambush had routed the force completely. An element from 4-50 ARVN Regiment reinforced the U.S. company and added five enemy bodies to the toll. No Americans were killed in the action.

In "Jitterbug" operations, the companies of the 2/60 Infantry on 18 March 1969 made nine insertions, no more than usual, and killed nineteen of the enemy while the air cavalry supporting the operation added sixteen. The contacts all occurred in the vicinity of the Bo Bo Canal in the Plain of Reeds, a major Viet Cong and NVA infiltration route. At one location seven enemy were killed and several detainees apprehended. Altogether, several weapons and a large quantity of ammunition were captured: 137 B-40 rockets, four AK-47 rifles, ten 107mm rocket rounds, five 57mm recoilless rifle rounds, and ninety-two chicom grenades.

During the 2/60 Infantry actions on 18 March, an estimated forty sampans had been spotted from the air. The sampans, some containing 55-gallon drums, had been sunk in the Bo Bo Canal to prevent detection. A thorough search of the surrounding area was made on the 19th and one of the largest caches ever found in the area was uncovered. Distributed in clusters over 400 meters, the cache contained: 400 Chicom grenades, 24,000 rounds of AK-47 ammunition, forty-seven 107mm rockets, twenty-five 57mm recoilless rifle rounds, ten 75mm RR rounds, 600 82mm mortar rounds, and forty B-40 rocket fuses.

In numerous actions like these, the division aggressively interdicted the enemy and slowly dried up his supplies. We also defeated infiltration groups of enemy troops. The Viet Cong's loss of supplies was noticeable in a salutary way: his attacks by fire against U.S. installations were reduced.

Table 11. 9th Infantry Division Quarterly Results of
Military Operations, 1967–1969

	1967			1968				1969	
	2	3	4	1	2	3	4	1	2
Enemy eliminated	1,998	1,604	1,207	3,336	3,409	2,671	3,249	7,107	8,138
Ratio: Enemy eliminated/ U.S. KHA	16.5	13.9	9.6	11.7	10.2	12.0	19.2	36.1	54.6

Source: 9th Infantry Division, Quarterly Operational Reports of 9th Infantry Division, April 1967–June 1969, Republic of Vietnam.

Measures of Success

As stated, the mission of the 9th Infantry Division was to destroy the Communist main and local force units and to directly support the GVN pacification program. The destruction of enemy units entailed not only the attrition of Communist forces but also the interdiction of the enemy infiltration of troops and materiel.

To attrit the enemy, we had to find him, and, in such a large area of responsibility, that required the daily commitment of many small-unit operations. On a quarterly basis, there were thousands of operations and hundreds of enemy contacts. Once a contact was made, there were several measures of military success. One was the total number of enemy eliminated, which included both those killed and captured. The division preferred to capture as many enemy as possible, not only for the intelligence obtained, but because it was more humane. Another measure was the exchange ratio, the number of enemy eliminated as compared to the number of U.S. soldiers killed by hostile action or the friendly efficiency. These two measures of military operations are shown on a quarterly basis in table 11; the large upsurge in both measures in 1969 is the subject of the table.

Since it was a guerrilla war, there were no boundaries; the enemy was everywhere, particularly in his so-called base areas. There were no front lines against which to measure progress, as in the World and Korean wars. However, since the goal of pacification was to establish

Fig. 17. Captured Viet Cong weapons

GVN presence in the thousands of hamlets and villages, it was important to provide security to those through military and civic actions. Therefore, the number of contested hamlets upgraded to secure status was a second measure of success. For that reason, the 9th Division always integrated combat operations with pacification efforts, attempting to upgrade hamlets to GVN control. In that respect, the course of pacification in 1968 and 1969 was substantially advanced in the division area by the upgrading of 217 out of 243 GVN targeted hamlets, 89 percent, a superb record. But more important, over 420,000 Vietnamese were freed from Viet Cong control.

Chapter 5

Third Phase of the VC/NVA General Offensive

At the beginning of August 1968, enemy operations were characterized by a general evasion of contact while maintaining large battalion-sized units in anticipation of a third offensive, with Saigon as the primary objective. In Long An Province—the underbelly of Saigon—enemy interdiction and guerrilla and terrorist activities were minimal, a good sign that offensive actions were imminent. Also in early August, the 1st Brigade captured a prisoner in Long An who identified his unit as the 520th Local Force Battalion from Kien Hoa Province. The displacement of a local force battalion from its home province was another indication that an offensive was coming. Additionally, the 294th NVA Battalion was dispersed in Long An to assist in the offensive, and a new VC unit, the 3rd Battalion, was identified.

Within a two-week period in August, the 1st Brigade had captured enemy soldiers from eight different battalions. Five of the seven VC battalions identified in the Mini-Tet attack from the south against Saigon were again attempting to mass for another attack. In just two months, these units had reconstituted. Obviously, their leadership had been weakened, and the new fillers were not as experienced. Nevertheless, they had left their base areas to assemble in Long An Province. Two more battalions were identified as assembling for the third phase than were involved in the May battles. A list of the Communist battalions involved in the Mini-Tet Offensive and those presumably attempting the third phase of the Communist General Offensive are listed in table 12.

In August, the 1st Brigade had so beaten up the Communists that several of their units were required to merge to maintain viable units. Prisoners informed us that the 294th NVA Battalion, by mid-August, had its strength reduced from six hundred to two hundred men. The NVA just didn't know the territory and suffered heavy losses.

Table 12. Communist Battalions Involved in General Offensives, 1968

Second phase (Mini-Tet)	Third phase (General Uprising)
Battle of Saigon, 8–13 May	August–September
5th Nha Be (AKA 6th Battalion)	6th Battalion (aka 5th Nha Be)
1st Long An Battalion	1st Long An Battalion
2nd Independent Battalion	2nd Independent Battalion
Phu Loi II Battalion	Dong Phu Battalion
265th Battalion	265th Battalion
252nd Battalion	——
502nd Battalion	——
	261st Battalion
	520th Battalion
	294th NVA Battalion
	3rd Battalion

The remnants of the battalion were assigned to the 1st Long An and 2nd Independent Battalions. The 5th Nha Be was ineffective and was absorbed by the 265th Battalion. Also, the Phu Loi II and Dong Nai Battalions were combined into the Dong Phu Battalion. These mergers were indicative that the VC were under great pressure and that recruiting to fill depleted ranks was becoming much more difficult. There was no doubt that the 1st Brigade had the VC on the run.

Under Col. Hank Emerson's leadership, the 1st Brigade perfected the seal-and-pile-on tactic and used it most successfully as they beat up one VC unit after another. Once an enemy force was detected by the air cavalry, often with People Sniffers, ground forces were quickly inserted to seal off the contact, and air support and artillery then pounded the encircled enemy.

On 7 August, two companies of the 6/31 Infantry Battalion made contact with an estimated VC Battalion eight kilometers southeast of Can Giuoc. Seven additional companies were inserted, encircling the enemy. Avenues of escape were cut off, and artillery was concentrated on the "doughnut" throughout the night. C-47 flareships provided continuous illumination of the area. A sweep the next morning yielded forty-six VC KIA, eleven POWs, and fourteen individual weapons and one crew-served weapon. Prisoners from the contact were from several different VC units: the 1st Long An, the 261 Battalion, and the Dong Phu Battalion.

On 12 August, C/5/60 Infantry engaged an enemy in Binh Phuoc District, and ten companies from the 2/39, 2/60, and 5/60 Infantry Battalions were inserted and encircled the enemy. The results of the contact were 104 VC KIA, 8 POWs, 2 Hoi Chanhs, and 21 individual and 5 crew-served weapons captured. Prisoners identified the engaged VC unit as the entire 520th Battalion. On 11 October 1968, Company C 2/39 Infantry overran VC Special Region 3 Forward Headquarters and captured a series of hand-drawn maps depicting recent battles that presumably were used to critique VC defenses against the 1st Brigade jitterbug and seal tactics. One of the maps was an after-action report entitled "Counter Operations of the 520 Battalion at Thuan My Village, 12 Aug 1968."[1] The map was well crafted, indicating important drainage and nipa palm areas. It shows the initial VC positions, including the location of the 520th Battalion headquarters. It also displays the 1st Brigade helicopter insertion sites and U.S. troops' subsequent maneuvers to encircle the enemy. It is extremely difficult to make an impenetrable encirclement covering such a large area, and, although in this case the enemy losses were substantial, some of them managed to break out. The enemy's routes of night withdrawal to the hamlet of Ap Dong Ninh are depicted. We subsequently learned that battalion-sized enemy units generally have a small reconnaissance unit whose duty is to probe our forces to find an opening for potential escape.

On 18 August, B/2/60 made contact in southwestern Can Giuoc District. Eight companies were inserted to encircle the unit. The battle resulted in ninety-three VC KIA, fifteen POWs, six Hoi Chanhs and forty-five weapons captured. Prisoners identified the unit as the 265th Battalion.

On 26 August, Hank Emerson and I were heading to a meeting in his command helicopter flying at about a thousand feet when a VC decided to take a potshot at the chopper, probably with an RPG. First, there was a loud explosion at the rear of the aircraft, and some seconds later there was a huge bang as the tail rotor came off and hit the side of the helicopter. Without the tail rotor, the helicopter precessed to the left and the pilots did their best to wrestle the aircraft down into a muddy, overgrown, isolated area. When the plane crashed, I was thrown out; and when I came to and looked about, I saw that one of the pilots and the brigade S-2 intelligence officer Capt. Jesse Decesare were out of the chopper. The plane was on its side, and flames were beginning to shoot up. Afraid that the chopper would "cook-off" any minute, Jesse and I ran to the side of the plane to see if we could help others. Hank Emerson was standing in the muck, his shirt on fire, and he was unable to unfasten his seat belt. So I unbuckled it for him and pulled him out. The pilot was dead, and the poor door gunner was buried in the muck underneath the aircraft. We were really out in the boonies, far from anything, and there was concern that the VC would find us soon. However, the alert S-2 had given a Mayday call over the radio on the way down, and the flames and smoke were billowing up several hundred feet, which enabled other helicopters to locate us. Colonel Emerson's arm was so badly burned that he had to be evacuated to the States, and the division commander put me in charge of the 1st Brigade while a replacement was found. I commanded the 1st Brigade from 26 August through 9 October, forty-five days.

The next day, C/2/39 made contact near Phuoc Lam, and prisoners indicated that elements of the 1st Long An and the 2nd Independent Battalions were engaged. On 30 August, in the same area, C/2/60 made contact again, and a prisoner identified his unit as the 1st Long An.

On 4 September, contact was made with a large VC unit that had fragmented into smaller segments dispersed in the same general area. Six companies from the 2/39, 2/60, and 5/60 were employed continuously through 6 September to destroy the enemy in a brigade seal and pile-on. The results were 131 VC KIA, 12 POWs, 1 Hoi Chanh, and 25 individual and 7 crew-served weapons captured.

In early September, one of our helicopters was shot down. Flying over the downed aircraft, I could see that the two pilots were still strapped in, probably unconscious from the impact. A small amount of smoke was noticeable coming from the aircraft, so, afraid that the chopper would catch fire and explode, I told my pilot to land. Then I made my way through the undergrowth and booby traps, intending to pull the pilots out. About ten yards from the burning plane, a heretofore unseen VC in a bunker (probably the one who shot down the plane) opened up at me. I fell into a depression in the ground, unable to move out because of the VC. After a minute or so, the helicopter exploded, raining small particles of molten metal everywhere. Subsequently, an infantryman worked his way behind the bunker and shot the VC. That night, I received a call from the Pentagon telling me to stand by for another call. Shortly afterward, my wife was on the phone saying, "Thank God you are alive!" Unbeknownst to me, a UP reporter accompanying the unit in contact that day had filed a report that I had been killed in action. That news was broadcast in the States on the morning television news shows, greatly upsetting my family. War is very hard on those who wait at home.

On 10 and 11 September, nine kilometers north of Rach Kien, elements of the 2/39 and 2/60 Battalions, in two separate reconnaissance-in-force operations, accounted for 78 VC KIA, 10 POWs, and 114 weapons captured, 96 of which were in a cache.

Again on 24–25 September, in another brigade seal and pile-on northwest of Rach Kien, five companies of the 2/60 and 2/39 Battalions encircled an enemy force while air strikes and artillery fire were placed on the enemy position. A sweep of the area yielded forty-two VC KIA, nine PW's, one Hoi Chanh, and fourteen weapons.

By this time, the Communists had abandoned any attempts to attack Saigon from the south. The major enemy units in Long An Province that were to have participated had been badly defeated, and the Viet Cong had again dispersed his units into smaller groups and was avoiding contact. Again, the 9th Division had foiled Communist efforts to implement the third phase of the General Offensive and General Uprising in our area.

The 9th Division seal-and-pile-on operations completely thwarted enemy intentions. The VC held high-level meetings whose purpose was to determine means to defeat our tactics. One such attempt was the plan to defeat Hawk tactics. In late September and early October, they tried another interesting solution: They would allow a small unit to be encircled and then, with other VC units some distance from the periphery, they would bring mortar and direct fire upon the encircling U.S. troops. Our gunships took care of the peripheral VC, and the encircled units were generally wiped out. So the VC had to go back to the drawing board!

The great value of the division headquarters' twice-daily intelligence briefings really became evident to me while in command of the 1st Brigade. As the result of months of these briefings, I was very aware of Viet Cong patterns of activities and was able to direct operations that very often made contact. As an example, there was a large overturned barge sunken at the shoreline of a major river which the VC would hide under, safe from aerial observation. They used it as a stopover for infiltrators coming into

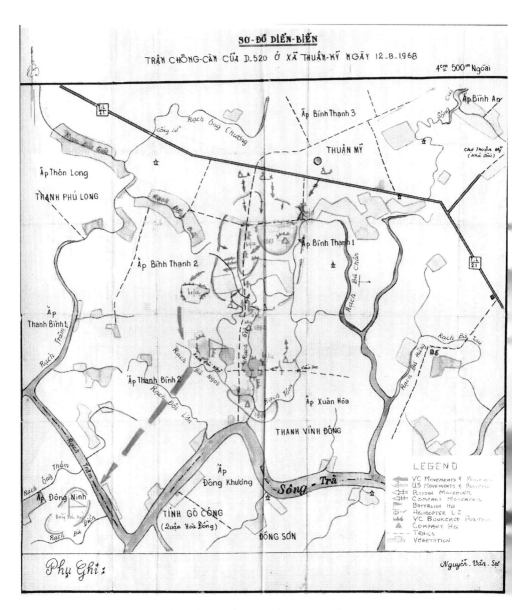

Map 2. Counter operations of 520th Battalion at Thuan My village, 12 August 1968

the area. About every ten days, I had the barge checked out, and invariably we would scarf up eight to ten Viet Cong. Many small contacts like this really added up to a large number of Viet Cong eliminated, but, more important, they kept our casualties down, since not so many insertions were required, reducing the risk of booby-trap injuries. Division statistics were published on a monthly basis, and for September, the ground troops of the 1st Brigade eliminated 502 Viet Cong, of which 44 were prisoners, with relatively few casualties. The 1st Brigade, you might say, was fortunate in that there were many more enemy in its area of operations, since the Viet Cong had massed in Long An to attempt the third-phase Offensive attack on Saigon. Overall, during my command, over twelve hundred enemy were eliminated by the brigade and supporting aviation units.

A fourth-quarter review indicated that the division's combat effectiveness continued to improve as the effects of management decisions and tactical innovations took root. Shortly after the end of each three-month period, the division held a quarterly commanders' conference to take stock of the situation. All aspects of divisional performance were reviewed. The G-3 would review the results of the combat operations of the previous three months, and the G-2 would give an update on the current enemy situation. During a mid-January 1969 conference, the G-3 reviewed combat operations for October through December 1968 to discern trends and determine what, if anything, needed to be tweaked to improve results. The first statistic reviewed was the exchange ratio, the number of enemy killed versus number of U.S. killed, a measure of friendly efficiency (see table 13). At 19.2 to 1, it was some 60 percent improved over the ratio of the previous nine months, a good sign. Since we always attempted to minimize casualties, we checked the U.S. KHAs per contact, which could be considered a measure of enemy effectiveness. At 0.19, it was only one-third the ratio of the previous quarter and an excellent sign that combat techniques were improving. The number of contacts, a direct correlation to the pressure placed on the enemy, had more than doubled the results of the previous two quarters. It was noted that the enemy losses per contact had decreased appreciably. This was considered the result of the enemy breaking down into much smaller units, but the statistic needed watching since it could be considered a measure of reduced friendly effectiveness. With all the efforts placed on unit and personnel management, it was gratifying to see that the number of operations, at 9,720, over 100 per day, had increased by 37

Table 13. 9th Infantry Division Quarterly Operational Reports, fourth quarter of 1967 through fourth quarter of 1968

Period	Operations	Contacts	Enemy eliminated*	U.S. forces killed in action	Enemy eliminated per contact for U.S. KHA	U.S. KHA per contact	Enemy eliminated per contact
1967 Fourth quarter		340	1,207	126	9.6	0.37	3.55
1968 First quarter	3,359	544	3,336	284	11.7	0.52	6.13
Second quarter	6,234	381	3,409	334	10.2	0.88	8.95
Third quarter	6,603	389	2,671	222	12.0	0.57	6.87
Fourth quarter	9,720	883	3,249	169	19.2	0.19	3.68

Source: Quarterly Operational Reports of 9th Infantry Division, April 1967–June 1969, Republic of Vietnam
Note: *Includes KIA (body count), POWs, Hoi Chanh, and VCI.

percent. But more important was that the number of contacts per operation had jumped 40 percent over the previous quarter's results.

A more detailed analysis of the 9,720 total operations indicated that 5,929, over 60 percent, were squad ambushes. Although these brave infantrymen made on the average only two contacts per day, they amounted to 19 percent of all contacts, slightly greater than platoon operational results. We learned early on that the retail concept of returns on operations, that is, a large number of small enemy eliminations, as compared to the wholesale concept, that is, to seek major enemy contacts, was the way to go. For example, if all thirty-nine companies would eliminate just one VC per day, that would amount to 1,170 per month, an amount, until December 1968, exceeded only twice in the previous twenty months, those during the Tet and Mini-Tet Offensives. By concentrating on keeping the pressure on the enemy over a large area night and day, the big contacts would come when we picked up enemy concentrations as they attempted to move to locations for a highpoint attack. Those sixty to seventy squad ambushes per day, almost always at night, enabled us to hit the local companies as they attempted to mortar our bases and to kill the enemy commo-liaison personnel as they were "carrying the mail." Company units had double the ratio of contacts to operations that platoon units did, and battalion operations doubled again the company results. This was, of course, due to two factors. First, the company and battalion commanders were more experienced leaders, and second, the companies and battalions were operating over a larger area. However, when results are looked at based upon an equivalent unit effort (i.e., three squads to a platoon, three platoons to a company), there was little difference among the outcomes of the squad, platoon, and company operations.

Teamwork is the essence of small-unit tactics, as illustrated by the actions of Private 1st Class Dunn and his platoon, as they outmaneuvered the enemy.

> On 15 March 1969, the continuous footmobile, airmobile, and watermobile operations, conducted by squads, platoons and companies both day and night, paid off handsomely for the Division on this date. No large contact was involved as 159 of the enemy fell to units under divisional control; rather, this day was ideally successful for the small unit tactics.
>
> Responsible for the success of these many small unit operations were individual acts such as those of Private First Class Gary E. Dunn, a rifleman with Company A, 4-39 Inf. The Company was making a reconnaissance-in-force when it came under heavy fire from an estimated enemy company; Dunn's platoon was directed to maneuver to the right to prevent an enemy flanking movement. Dunn volunteered to walk point and was thirty-five meters ahead of his platoon, making his way through the dense nipa, when he spotted an enemy squad setting up an ambush directly in front of him. Reacting quickly, Dunn killed two of the would-be ambushers and other platoon members killed two more as the enemy fled. Without the cool professionalism and bravery of Dunn and thousands of infantrymen, displayed day after day in similar situations, many American soldiers would have died unnecessarily.

Unquestionably, the pace of operations was increasing and the number of contacts per operation was improving. Over the previous nine months, the division had averaged more than a hundred POWs captured per month; they, with the Hoi Chanhs, were excellent sources of information as to the enemy's strengths, locations, and habits.

Considering the concept of constant pressure, one area of concern was the nighttime output. To get a handle on that situation, in December 1968 the division started keeping statistics on five categories of operations: day infantry, day air cavalry, others (which included artillery,

Table 14. 9th Infantry Division, Enemy Eliminated, Day and Night, 1968–1969

	December 1968	January 1969	February 1969	March 1969	April 1969	May 1969
Day						
Air Calvary	398	341	337	571	429	516
Infantry	399	557	749	1,191	1,379	1,084
Other	124	146	157	377	340	485
Total	921	1,044	1,243	2,140	2,148	2,085
Night						
Air Calvary	34	143	391	580	355	266
Infantry	153	248	315	1,003	807	496
Total	187	391	706	1,583	1,162	762
Total, day and night	1,108	1,435	1,949	3,723	3,310	2,847
Ratio, night/total	0.17	0.27	0.36	0.43	0.35	0.27

Source: 9th Infantry Division, Quarterly Commanders' Conferences, April 1967–June 1969, Republic of Vietnam.

Air Force, et cetera), night infantry, and night air cavalry (see table 14). In December, the total daytime eliminations were 921, and nighttime eliminations were 187, or 17 percent of the total. To ratchet up the pressure on the enemy, we had to improve night operations. However, two of our latest tactical innovations were just coming on line: the Night Search and the sniper program. The Night Search technique had been successfully tested in late December and in early January. The current aircraft operational ready rate was such that it could support several Night Searches an evening. With respect to the sniper program, the second class graduated in early December so that there was a full complement of snipers assigned to each of the battalions. The operational aspects of these assignments had been fine-tuned, and field results were already improving. It was believed that those two techniques would greatly improve nighttime results and pay big dividends by keeping constant pressure on the enemy.

The G-2 briefed the intelligence situation in mid-January 1969: after the Viet Cong's second abortive offensive in May and his third highpoint attempt in August–September, the enemy units in the Upper Delta withdrew to their base areas to regroup while COSVN rethought its strategy. To avoid detection, the enemy broke into small groups and attempted to mingle with the population where possible. Communist main force units were severely depleted in both men and materiel and

Fig. 18. Taking ten

would have to be resupplied, usually in small movements to avoid detection. Evidence of increasing infiltration along the Vam Co Tay River and Bo Bo Canal and through the Plain of Reeds continued to accumulate. It was believed once the main force units were back to strength that they would attempt to stage another highpoint. The Viet Cong targets were always the same: Saigon, provincial capitals like Tan An and Ben Tre; major cities such as My Tho, Cai Lay, and Mo Cay; and U.S. and RVNAF military installations, particularly Dong Tam and the 7th ARVN Division headquarters at My Tho. The Viet Cong, always offensively oriented, in the interim between highpoints would periodically have local force units carry out attacks by fire against the aforementioned targets. Breaking down into smaller units complicated the enemy's command and control and necessitated an increase in the use of communications liaison personnel. Their use of radio would be kept to a minimum except in emergencies.

The enemy order of battle on 20 December 1968 in the Fourth Military Region included five regimental headquarters, fourteen main force battalions, seventeen local force battalions, fifteen main force companies, eighty-two local force companies, and eight local force platoons, for a total of 44,777 combatants. This did not include the NVA/VC units in our heavily enemy-infested area surrounding Saigon from the south.²

At the conclusion of the quarterly commanders' conference, which presented a careful review of the situation at year's end, Major General Ewell decided that the division would continue to do more of the same. The additional air assets received from IV Corps for the Dry Weather Campaign would allow each brigade to conduct daily jitterbugging, thus improving our daytime operations, and the Night Search and sniper innovations would accelerate nighttime results. The concept of operations was simply to maintain a constant pressure on the enemy night and day, with the objective to prevent him from conducting his Dong Xuan Winter-Spring Offensive by intercepting his infiltration of men and materials and by attriting his forces so that he was prevented from massing for a highpoint attack. In this manner, the countryside would become more secure and pacification efforts would improve.

Chapter 6

Fourth Phase of the VC/NVA General Offensive

The division captured an enemy document in January 1969 that indicated that the fourth phase of the General Offensive and General Uprising, the Dong Xuan, a Winter-Spring Offensive, was imminent. Its objectives were to annihilate 60 percent of the enemy troops and destroy 50 percent of the enemy outposts; liberate the rural areas and attack the enemy lines of communication; and liberate half of the district seats and provincial capitals and destroy the remaining half so that they could eventually control them all. In fact, a Viet Cong supply convoy was interdicted in Kien Phong Province on 13 January, a few days prior to the quarterly conference, and a twelve-tube 107 mm rocket launcher with forty-five 107 mm rocket rounds and other supplies and ammunition were captured. Other new weapons and equipment taken by the division further indicated serious Viet Cong preparations for a new highpoint offensive.

The goals for the Dong Xuan changed but little in the forthcoming years. It was always the main Communist objective to defeat the GVN pacification program and to gain control of land and population, that is, "liberate the rural areas." It wasn't until December 1974 that the Communists managed to capture a provincial capital, Phuoc Binh, the capital of Phuoc Long Province, seventy-five miles northeast of Saigon.

Additional intelligence indicated that an NVA regiment was to be introduced into Long An Province and that NVA troop replacements would beef up the depleted VC main force units. The conflict south of Saigon was becoming a VC/NVA war. We also learned that two new VC battalions had been formed—the 560th Battalion in Kien Hoa and the 273rd Battalion in Dinh Tuong. Several reorganizations of the enemy forces were also made, including the formation of the 1st Battle Group to control the enemy battalions in Kien Hoa and the consolidation of several mortar and rocket artillery units under the control of the Ben Duc artillery headquarters. Thus, the evidence was unmistakable that the enemy planned to make a major effort to attack population centers and disrupt the pacification program in the Upper Delta.

The enemy order of battle indicated that the division in its area was faced with four enemy regimental headquarters, twelve main force and local force battalions, and at least as many local force companies supported by thousands of guerrillas, all of whom were recruiting, training, and resupplying main force units for planned attacks in a massive Winter-Spring Offensive to destroy populated areas and inflict high casualties on Allied Forces to weaken the people's loyalty to the GVN and thus gain adherents, which would influence negotiations at the Paris peace conference.

The Communists' plan for a Winter-Spring Offensive coincided with the IV Corps Tactical Zone's Dry Weather Campaign, whose objective was the obverse of the enemy's; that is, to destroy enemy forces, clear base areas, and reduce the enemy's capability to sustain operations by interdicting reinforcements and resupply activities, thereby greatly supporting the 1969 pacification and development plan.

Thus, by mid-January 1969 all of the division's building blocks began to fall into place. It took over eight months of hard work, analyses, management decisions, and innovations. Again, in May 1968 the division initiated a two-pronged effort to enhance its operational capabilities; one of these was to provide the maximum number of healthy, well-equipped, and properly supported combat soldiers to the field on a daily basis. By December, the infantry battalions had been converted from three to four companies, and the paddy strength requirements were being met. We had transferred infantrymen with incapacitating foot problems, and, as the result of Operation Safe Step, in October a directive was issued limiting combat operations in the paddies to forty-eight hours, thus preventing additional foot problems. We had thirty-five hundred healthy, aggressive infantrymen in the field daily. Next to the combat soldiers, our most important asset was aircraft.

We established a maintenance program to ensure that the maximum number of aircraft were operationally ready on a daily basis, and through analysis we greatly increased aircraft utilization and operational flexibility. Finally, in December, the maintenance hangars at

Dong Tam were completed, facilitating all-night maintenance, thus providing the additional aircraft necessary for the new night aviation tactics. Not only did the helicopters provide firepower and maneuverability in the inundated Delta, enabling the infantrymen to clobber the Viet Cong, but, when aviation assets supplemented the soldiers, combat casualties were greatly reduced. Another vital asset was the complete integration of intelligence and operational efforts. After the move to Dong Tam, the G-2 improved the agent nets, and after several months of cooperative effort with the RVNAF units, there were meaningful exchanges of information. By December, the ICAPs were providing excellent information that could be acted upon. We utilized sensors to the maximum, constantly collating and disseminating data from side-looking airborne radar, infrared emissions, and divisional radar and intrusion devices, attempting when possible to respond to meaningful intelligence reports with rapid reactions.

The second effort was to improve combat capabilities through improved performance in the field. This was accomplished by adjusting tactics to the terrain and the enemy. We continually improved jitterbug techniques. Over time, we greatly reduced the insertion distances from the targets without the loss of men or helicopters. We asked and received permission to insert with five choppers instead of ten, which allowed us to cover more intelligence targets, and we refined the seal-and-pile-on technique. More units adopted the Bushmaster and Checkerboard tactics and, once they mastered them, used smaller units in order to cover a greater area. Ambushes became an art with stay-behind groups and the novel uses of surveillance equipment such as pink filter Xenon searchlights and night observation devices. Troops incorporated radar and intrusion devices into their ambush plans. With sheer guts, infantrymen established ambushes in and near VC base areas. Finally, in January the division sniper program started clicking. Snipers were used on Tango boats, as spotters on Night Searches, and as the key element in ambushes. The snipers' expertise and experience raised the confidence of their units so that the division had as many soldiers in the field at night as during the day. Night raids had a psychological impact on the VC. However, the most important tactical innovation was the evolution of the Night Search technique. This enabled the division to cover suspected enemy infiltration routes over large areas both night and day. It dramatically increased the number of enemy killed while greatly reducing casualties. Most important, it enabled the division to fully implement the concept of constant pressure.

The division avidly monitored night operations (see table 14). After several Night Search operations, we were able to improve the technique by utilizing a stabilized night observation device instead of the spotter's starlight scope. Also, the spotters became much more skilled with experience, and the operations, which originated with the 1st Brigade, were adopted by the other two brigades, thereby expanding their number of operations. The success of the Night Search operations continued to increase, peaking in March with 477 enemy eliminated (see table 7). Sniper results rapidly improved thereafter, peaking with an astonishing 346 kills in April (see table 6). The success of the snipers' night ambushes raised the confidence of all units, and night infantry operations improved many fold. In March, 43 percent of all enemy eliminated was at night, and over half of the night kills were by Night Search and sniper operations.

In early January, the last building block finally fell into place. The IV Corps' Dry Weather Campaign allocated the division another air assault company and another air cavalry troop on a daily basis. Thus, for the first time, each brigade had air assets on a daily basis (twenty-four days per month). What a difference; all brigades were pulling equally. Almost every day, all provinces were subject to daytime air mobile assaults and Night Searches.

An important element in our successful day and night operations was the capability of our commanders to utilize all of the division's available assets in the conduct of combined area operations, including artillery, gunships, and organic weapons.

> Farther south, the 2d Brigade's Mobile Riverine Forces added eight VC to the day's total. Friendly casualties in the Brigade were fifteen wounded and one killed; four of the wounded resulted from booby traps. Captain Paul Blackwell's heroic actions stood out during the day's fighting by the 2d Brigade. While his company deployed in a night location, they came under heavy fire. The initial burst killed a platoon leader and seriously wounded a platoon sergeant. Upon hearing the fire and learning of the casualties, Captain Blackwell immediately called for artillery and directed his men to withdraw to more secure positions. Blackwell then called for gunships and directed his forward observer to continue artillery fire until the gun-

Fig. 19. Constant muck and water

ships arrived. He directed the gunship fire onto the enemy positions and combined this skillfully with organic weapons and artillery to rout enemy,. Throughout the conflict, Captain Blackwell exposed himself to enemy fire and displayed awesome personal courage. His actions inspired his men to decisive action and his skill in coordinating combined arms held his own casualties down.

Thus, by mid-January, with all the pieces fitting together, the 9th Division was ready for take-off.

Chapter 7

The Take-off

By the end of the first quarter in 1969, the effectiveness of combat operations had peaked, preempting Communist efforts. The brave soldiers of the division displayed extraordinary heroism in conducting more than one hundred offensive operations daily, half of which were at night, in the extremely difficult and treacherous booby-trapped terrain; this resulted in over thirty contacts per day, eliminating thousands of Viet Cong. Almost all of the contacts were minor skirmishes, keeping a constant pressure on the evading enemy. However, during this exploratory period there were five major battles, which severely punished the Viet Cong and NVA main force units. Although these major contacts contributed less than 10 percent of the enemy losses, they were vital in diminishing the enemy's command and control apparatus.

The review of these battles that follows vividly illustrates the techniques and tactics of the division, including airmobile assault (jitterbugging), seal and pile-on, ambushes, gunship, artillery and Air Force firepower, Night Searches, snipers, Tiger Scouts, RVNAF cooperation, usefulness of POWs and Hoi Chanhs, radar sightings, People Sniffers, and more.

When elements of the 3rd Brigade in Long An Province met and defeated the K-6 Battalion, 1st NVA Regiment, on 25–26 January, it initiated a period of unprecedented success brought about by the gallantry of the 9th Infantry Division soldiers. The unrelenting pressure of the division and its South Vietnamese allies crushed the Communist forces in the Upper Delta, inflicting defeat after defeat upon the hapless enemy, such as in the Battle of Phu My.

> The 3rd Brigade "Go Devils," on 25 January 1969, encountered fierce enemy resistance in a two-day battle. The contact was initiated by a Long Range Reconnaissance Patrol from Company E, 75th Infantry (Ranger).

They had been inserted by helicopter into a Landing Zone seven miles west of Tan An at approximately 1145 hrs on the 25th. As the patrol cautiously approached a nearby woodline, an abrupt fusillade of automatic weapons fire raked their position. The volume of fire indicated that an enemy force of at least a company was concealed in the tangled growth of nipa palm. Staff Sergeant Thayer, the patrol leader, aggressively maneuvered his tiny unit in a bold attempt to even the odds. Even after he was wounded, Sergeant Thayer repeatedly braved a hail of bullets to call in supporting fire in his dogged determination to win. Thayer, disregarding his physical pain, remained in control of his team to supervise the safe evacuation of wounded members of his patrol.

Another patrol member, Specialist Bellwood, alertly spotted and killed a Viet Cong who had leaped from a spider hole and was firing at the team from point blank range. Disregarding his personal safety, Bellwood then engaged and killed another enemy soldier who was trying to maneuver against the team, only to be fatally wounded by a sniper's bullet.

After the LRRP's had been extracted from the area, two companies of 5-60 Infantry and three companies from 2-60 Infantry were deployed in reaction to the contact. Supporting fire from D/3-5 Cavalry, Tactical Air, and artillery pounded the area, while the infantry was inserted to seal off and entrap the enemy. Company D, 5-60 Infantry was inserted and became embroiled in savage contact as darkness approached. Three more companies from 2-60 Infantry were airmobiled into the fray, tightening the noose around the now completely encircled enemy. The Air Force's "Spooky" flareship and helicopter gunships employing spotlights illuminated the battle area to reveal any attempt by the enemy to elude the trap, while artillery saturated the enemy's positions with its awesome firepower. Air strikes were called in the next morning to further pulverize the beleaguered foe. Close on the heels of the tactical air strikes, the "Old Reliables" of the 3rd Brigade swept the area, encountering numerous enemy dead strewn across the battlefield. After the sweep, airmobile "Jitterbug" operations continued in the areas surrounding the contact in an effort to reestablish contact with the fleeing remnants of the enemy force.

Sergeant Prance, Vickers' RTO, instinctively assumed command of the company and began deploying its elements to meet the changing situation. Prance moved to a forward position to better control the company and enlist the aid of artillery and tactical air strikes. Throughout the battle, Sergeant Prance continued his heroic efforts, directing the fire and maneuver of the platoons and insuring that casualties were evacuated.

The turning point in the battle resulted from the combined efforts of the ground troops and the supporting elements. Indicative of this teamwork was the action and gallantry displayed by 1st Lt Cozzalio, a gunship pilot from D Troop, 3-5 Cavalry. While flying in support of Company C, 5-60 Infantry, Cozzalio spotted the enemy positions that were being marked by Lt Vickers. Cozzalio landed his gunship and commandeered a more versatile Light Observation Helicopter in order to better attack the target. With gallant disregard for his own safety Cozzalio hovered a few feet above the enemy positions and engaged them initially with CS gas and then with his "mini-gun," killing two of the four enemy beneath him. When the bunker was effectively neutralized, Cozzalio landed, briefed the infantry leader on the situation as seen from above, and then guided the maneuver force into the enemy position. As a result of these and many other heroic actions, the enemy was routed and heavy casualties inflicted upon him. A sweep of the battle area revealed 78 enemy killed.

POWs captured during the Battle of Phu My identified the unit as the K-6 Battalion, 1st NVA Regiment. This was the division's first encounter with an NVA unit since August and indicated that, to carry out the Communist Winter-Spring Offensive, the Viet Cong MR-2 units had to be reinforced by NVA troops. The POWs stated that the whole 1st NVA Regiment, consisting of the K-4, K-5, and K-6 Battalions, was in Long An Province with the mission to attack the provincial capital of Tan An and U.S. elements. Subsequently, the 9th Division captured POWs from all three battalions of the 1st NVA Regiment.

The validity of the threat assessment of an impending attack on Saigon from Long An Province was corroborated by the debriefs of POWs captured from several VC units in the same time frame. On the same day as the Phu My contact, four POWs from the 265th Battalion were captured in the vicinity of Can Guioc while on a reconnaissance mission. A few days later, on 29 January, a POW from the 211th Sapper Battalion was captured in the vicinity of Tan Tru. He said his battalion, along with the 1st Long An and the Dong Phu Battalions, was going to attack Saigon in the near future.

Viet Cong preparations for the Winter-Spring Offensive were also ongoing in other areas of the division TAOI. In Ding Tuong Province, a POW captured on 27 January stated that the Hau My guerrillas had been ordered to prepare bunkers for a major Viet Cong unit that was soon to arrive in the area. Additionally, the guerrillas were told to prepare rice for two thousand Viet Cong. The division's agent network was actively receiving many reports that the Viet Cong were preparing for attacks by fire against Dong Tam, My Tho, and ARVN facilities. The second major fight, the Battle of Thanh Loi, was initiated by a 3rd Brigade radar sighting of a large enemy movement.

> Infantrymen from the 2-60 Infantry of 3rd Brigade, along with gunships from 3-17 Cavalry, engaged an enemy force fifteen kilometers north of Tan An in an action on 1 February 1969 that resulted ultimately in sixty-three enemy dead. Contact had begun the day before when an element of the battalion conducting sweep operations engaged an enemy force of unknown size. Two more companies were inserted as the contact developed. During the ensuing exchange, the infantrymen killed thirty-nine and the gunships accounted for twenty-four enemy casualties. The action was initiated by a radar sighting at Brigade Headquarters. It appeared that a lucrative target would develop and elements of 2-60 Infantry were inserted at the location in the Plain of Reeds. The friendly force soon drew fire from an enemy force determined to be at least company-sized. The remaining two companies of 2-60 Infantry "piled on" and soon the enemy force was encircled. Artillery and gunships poured in heavy fire upon the enemy position. A sweep of the area on the 2nd of February revealed that sixty-three enemy soldiers, identified as North Vietnamese of the 4010 Infiltration Group, had been killed. Twenty-seven small arms and seven crew-served weapons were captured. During this two-day encounter, the 3rd Brigade suffered only two U.S. killed and five wounded. In this action, Private First Class Rodney L. Muniz displayed the heroism that makes military success possible. Muniz crawled alone toward a bunker from which withering fire had pinned down his comrades and himself. Reaching the bunker, PFC Muniz stuffed two grenades through the firing port and destroyed the fortification, killing its occupants. His heroic action epitomized the courage and loyalty which enabled his company and his entire brigade to continue its mission.

An intercepted high-level Communist message dictated an aggressive Dong Xuan (Winter-Spring Offensive), whose purpose was to influence the ongoing Paris peace negotiations. This was a replay of the Tet

Offensive where the VC/NVA, although they were soundly defeated, had gained political notoriety. Intelligence indicated that the Communists were convinced that a major military offensive was necessary to bolster their efforts at Paris. In our area, all sources indicated an increase in enemy activities whose purpose, as revealed in captive documents, was to annihilate enemy troops, liberate rural areas, attack lines of communication, and capture half of the district seats and provincial capitals.

COSVN broadcast that the Viet Cong unilaterally were going to observe a truce for a week during the Tet holidays, 15–22 February—they had used this subterfuge to carry out all-out surprise attacks at Tet 1968. It was obvious to the division that preparations for a Viet Cong highpoint were in progress and this was a good opportunity to interdict major Viet Cong units as they assembled to carry out offensive operations. The 2nd Brigade in Kien Hoa Province was particularly aggressive in patrolling its area to disrupt enemy preparations for the suspected Viet Cong highpoint, which resulted in the Battle of Ap Binh Dong.

> Intelligence sources in Kien Hoa revealed that civilian laborers were being forced to assist the Viet Cong units there in their pre-offensive movement of supplies. Reports indicated that the 516, 560, and 550 Battalions along with the 550th Local Force Company would be used in the attack on Ben Tre City.
>
> At 15 0600 hrs February 1969, the Viet Cong truce began and was broadcast to last until 22 0600 hrs February. It was concluded that the Viet Cong had nearly completed preparations for their offensive. Their build-up was undoubtedly delayed and hampered by the 9th Infantry Division operations, which continued to exact a heavy toll from the enemy units within the Division TAOI. A decidedly damaging blow was dealt the enemy's capability in Kien Hoa Province during a 2nd Brigade contact on 20 February.
>
> The searching, probing tactics of the 2nd Brigade paid big dividends on 20 February when the Mobile Riverine Force brought the 516th Viet Cong Main Force Battalion to bay and laced into them, killing ninety-nine. Action began when Company C, 3-47 Infantry, on a combined operation with the 126th Regional Force Company, received sporadic fire as they moved through an area along the Ba Lai River, northwest of Giong Trom. Shortly thereafter, Troop D, 3-5 Cavalry, brought in a prisoner who said that he was a member of the 516th and that the battalion was deployed in

full force along the Ba Lai River. He stated further that the unit was splitting into two groups, one moving north and the other moving east along the river. Company C, 3-47 Infantry, immediately undertook a search and destroy mission to interdict the element moving east. No contact was made immediately, so the company decided to push further east. Suddenly, they began to receive sniper fire.

At 1115 hrs, helicopters from D/3-5 Cavalry were screening the front of Company C when they received automatic weapons fire from the junction of the Rach Cau Pheng and the Rach Ba Tri Rom (XS686262). Artillery and Air Force jets were called in to support, but the enemy fire persisted, downing one cavalry helicopter.

Company B, 3-60 Infantry, made an airmobile assault to the northeast of the stream junction, and the helicopters came under heavy fire as they lifted off following insertion of the infantrymen. Charlie Company, 3-47 Infantry, remained in a blocking position west of the stream junction along the Ba Lai River. The 126th RF Company moved along the trail adjacent to Company C, also to set up a blocking position, in this case, to the east.

At 1453 hrs, B/3-47 Infantry made a heliborne assault to the south of the stream junction and were engaged immediately by heavy automatic weapons fire. It was apparent at this time that the enemy force was of a considerable size. The company commander and one platoon leader were killed shortly after the insertion and the enemy began pumping in 60mm mortar rounds. Realizing their precarious position, the men of Bravo Company returned a heavy column of fire with their organic weapons and inched toward the enemy entrenchments, eliminating the enemy one by one.

"We were surrounded, so we hit the dikes and canals for cover," said SP4 Phil Barile, Bravo Company radio-telephone operator. "They had snipers all around us, so we started putting out as much M-60 machine gun fire as we could. Then, with the help of the Cav, we moved out to get them."

At 1640 hrs, B/3-60 Infantry was reinserted, this time to the left flank of B/3-47 Infantry and south of the stream junction. Upon insertion, they also came under heavy enemy fire, but this move sealed off the cordon to the south and west. Company A, 3rd Battalion, 47th Infantry, was inserted at 1810 hrs to the right flank of B/3-47 to seal off the escape routes to the east along the Rach Ba Tri Rom. Company C, in its blocking position, now became the ready reaction force.

By 1850 hrs, all three companies were still in heavy contact with the entrenched enemy, whose defensive line was now defined as running east and west generally along the Rach Cau Pheng and Rach Ba Tri Rom. The enemy, displaying unusually heavy firepower, kept the infantrymen under a blanket of .50 caliber and mortar fire. Although low on ammunition, Bravo Company, 3-47 Infantry, continued its fierce close-in combat. They were not intimidated by the enemy's fortifications and the three .50 caliber machine guns which raked their position from no more than fifty meters away. As night fell, however, the enemy positions had been pin-pointed and all friendly fires coordinated. Delta Troops, 3-5 Cavalry, screened the northern flank of the cordon. Now it was the enemy's lot to feel the sting of artillery, as Battery C, 3-34 Artillery, pummeled the center of the cordon all through the night with hundreds of 105 mm howitzer rounds. Again and again the enemy tried to break the noose forcefully, but the infantrymen and artillery pushed him back.

At first light on 21 February, the infantrymen swept the area, assaulting the remaining enemy pockets of resistance. Intelligence gathered on the battlefield and reports of the local populace revealed that the enemy force had been composed of the 1st and 2nd Companies, 516th Main Force Battalion, and included the Battalion Command Post and a reinforced heavy weapons platoon. The base camp of the 516th was also completely obliterated.

The sweep revealed fifty-four enemy bodies, bringing the total of known enemy kills for the action to ninety-nine. Seven 9th Division soldiers lost their lives in the bitter fighting, and ten were wounded, almost all of these in the initial stages of the battle.

The Communists held to their announced truce. Cleverly, they used this one-week truce period to attempt to maneuver units into positions for attacks on their objectives. In Long An, a major NVA infiltration group, which had been sent to reinforce VC units in preparation for the attack on Saigon, had been intercepted and defeated. In Dinh Tuong, our agents had reported that VC units were preparing to attack major installations, and the reports were verified by prisoners from several different VC units. In Kien Hoa, the Communists established the 1st Battle Group to coordinate and control the Kien Hoa VC battalions preparing for the forthcoming highpoint. All indications were that the VC/NVA were definitely going to initiate a major offensive in the 9th Division area.

On the evening of 22 February, at the conclusion of the one-week

VC-declared truce over the Tet holidays, throughout South Vietnam there was a large surge of intense VC attacks by fire against population centers and military installations. In the 9th Division area, the largest attacks by fire were against My Tho and Dong Tam; each received about a hundred rounds of mortar fire. According to POWs and captured documents, the highpoint activities were verified subsequent to 22 February. A captured high-ranking former political officer of the 6th VC Battalion, Senior Captain Xang, stated that the general offensive was to kick off at 2200 hrs on 22 February. Another POW captured on 23 February just north of My Tho said that three companies of the 550th Battalion from Kien Hoa had crossed the My Tho River to reinforce the 514th A Battalion and the 263rd Battalion for a major attack against My Tho on 22 February. A Hoi Chanh from the 267th B Battalion substantiated this, stating that the 267th B Battalion, along with the 263th Local Battalion, the 514th A Battalion, and local force units, were ordered to attack My Tho. However, they said the attack was called off because of coordination problems, since the battalions involved had not reached their attack positions. This was to have been a major coordinated attack with at least four main force VC units, equaling the VC efforts against My Tho in Tet 1968. There was no question but that the interdiction efforts of the 7th ARVN Division and the 9th Infantry Division delayed the VC units, requiring them to abort their plan. On 24 February, a VC document captured in Long An verified that the highpoint of the Winter-Spring Offensive would commence on the night of 22 February and would be conducted in three phases, lasting five, ten, and nineteen days each. The enemy fully intended to continue to execute the objectives of the Dong Xuan previously outlined. The Communist immediate post-Tet 1969 objectives were effectively preempted by Allied Forces, and it was very important that the Division continue to interdict the NVA/VC in their attempts to achieve some military advantages in order to bolster their bargaining position at the Paris peace negotiations.

At this time, Col. John Geraci, the outstanding commander of the 1st Brigade, had a family emergency that required his immediate attention. When he rotated home, the division commander again directed me to take over the 1st Brigade until a replacement was available. On this occasion, I commanded the brigade for nineteen days, from 22 February through 12 March 1969.

In August and September 1968, I had assumed command at the height of the Communist third phase of the General Offensive and Uprising, and on 22 February, I assumed command at the height of the fourth phase. The current situation was somewhat different, in that many unit leaders and troops had rotated and the 1st Brigade area of responsibility was now Dinh Tuong Province instead of Long An Province. Tactics too had evolved. The Night Search, which had been initiated by Colonel Geraci, and the full complement of trained snipers really gave the brigade the capabilities to ratchet up the pressure on the Viet Cong at night. The constant around-the-clock pressure was beginning to hurt the enemy badly. Nonetheless, the Communists were at it again, attempting to get something going during this critical Winter-Spring Offensive.

During my first week in command, I noted several factors. The air cavalry was not utilizing the People Sniffer as much as they had in the past, and they were requested to do so. More important, in the first week, the battalions had only executed five Night Search operations. For the Viet Cong to carry out their current offensive plan, they desperately needed ammunition and weapons, and they were aggressively attempting to infiltrate them from sanctuaries in Cambodia and from Base Area 470 in western Dinh Tuong Province. This, then, was certainly the time to increase the Night Search and Night Ambushes along the canals and rivers to cut off the infiltration. Since I monitored the division's aircraft maintenance and availability, I knew that aircraft assets were available for two or three daily night operations. I alerted division headquarters to expect increased requests for night aviation assets. Between 1 and 12 March, the brigade conducted twenty-three nighttime airmobile operations, eighteen Night Searches and five Night Raids, over three times the rate of the previous week. Previously, I had thoroughly discussed the concept of the Night Raid with Captain Hudson, S-2 of the 2/39 Infantry Battalion, and at that time encouraged its implementation. Commencing on 4 March, the 2/39 Infantry Battalion carried out five of these most daring operations. Sadly, Captain Hudson was killed on 17 March. These night operations really hit the Viet Cong hard, resulting in a great number of enemy eliminations. During the nineteen days of my command, the 1st Brigade and its supporting units, in numerous contacts, as illustrated here, eliminated over 1,000 Viet Cong and had only seven soldiers killed.

> Squads, platoons and companies of the 1st Brigade flooded the area to establish contact and destroy the enemy in a piecemeal fashion. Occasionally, a larger Viet Cong force exposed itself. On 6 March, elements of the 1st Brigade detected and practically eliminated the 4th Company of the 514 C Battalion at My Hanh Trung Village in northern Dinh Tuong Province. The contact begun by a sharp-eyed 191st Assault Helicopter Company pilot resulted in forty-three enemy dead and disrupted the meeting of the VC Dinh Tuong area command. "We spotted an individual with a weapon in an open rice paddy," said Warrant Officer Mike Holt, the gunship pilot. "At first, I thought he might be an ARVN soldier, but when we went down to check him out, he jumped into the water. We were only fifty feet away when he fired a burst at us, smashing the chin bubble and sun visor. My door gunner reacted fast and killed him."

During the day on 6 March, the 1st Brigade also eliminated another sixty-four enemy in a large number of small and scattered contacts. This constant attrition was definitely sapping the enemy's strength, both in manpower and equipment. Yet the Communists doggedly continued to seek a military victory. On 11–12 March 1969, elements of the 1st Brigade made contact with a large VC force at Thanh Phu, several kilometers from My Phuoc Tay and reported seventy-two VC KIA killed in the battle.

> Prior to midday, C/2-39 Infantry had not been able to establish contact with the enemy during "Jitterbug" insertions. Several intelligence targets had been checked out and found devoid of enemy when the battalion commander decided to investigate an area along the Kinh Tong Doc Luc Canal near the hamlet of My Phuoc Tay. The Airborne Personnel Detector, or "People Sniffer," in the air cavalry troop command and control helicopter had obtained a significantly high reading over the area. GS gas was used to flush out the enemy but no movement was detected, so a platoon from the company was inserted and moved cautiously toward a line of bunkers. Cobra gunships engaged a few Viet Cong in the bunkers, but started a grass fire which grew and, rekindled elsewhere by subsequent rockets and air strikes, lasted all day. In the later stages of the battle, the smoke and fire

detracted from the ability of gunship pilots and forward air controllers to support the ground troops, whose forward locations were often invisible to the pilots. The platoon approached through a booby-trapped area to within fifteen meters of the bunkers before coming under a fusillade of enemy fire. The enemy force was obviously too large for the infantry platoon, which attempted to withdraw. Several men of the platoon were injured during this withdrawal through booby traps and mines. The gunships were unable to suppress the enemy fire because the action was now taking place under a cloud of smoke. Another platoon from C/2-39 Infantry was inserted to the south of the first and assisted in the withdrawal of the beleaguered platoon and the evacuation of its casualties. Because of the smoke, casualties, and confusion, the decision was made to extract the elements of C/2-39 Infantry, but in the meantime, instructions had been given to ready several other companies for insertion around the enemy position. Artillery pieces were being moved into position to support the ground troops and Air Force forward air controllers were in position to guide air strikes.

The immediate goal was to encircle the enemy positions, to seal him in a "doughnut" of American troops. Artillery, air strikes and gunships could then be used to pound the center. Insertions were planned, accordingly, to cut off the enemy escape routes. This meant, first, the placement of troops either side of the bunkered positions, which lay along an east-west canal. As the insertions took place, artillery and gunship fire and air strikes were placed all around the enemy to contain him. South of the canal B/2-39 Infantry was placed on the ground at 1415 hrs to block the canal on the east. Ten utility helicopters inserted A/2-39 Inf on the west at 1511 hrs. Shortly after 1630 hrs, C/6-31 Inf was airlifted into the center, where the initial contact had been made. All three companies moved toward positions along the canal, but found the going very tough. Mines and booby traps were everywhere and the Viet Cong reacted with well-placed fire from small arms, automatic weapons and mortars. Some timely air strikes assisted the advance greatly, however, by leveling the area to the front and causing many of the booby traps to detonate prematurely.

Attention was then shifted to the north of the canal. Though relatively wide and deep, the canal could not be considered a natural barrier and, unless prevented, the Viet Cong could be expected to make their escape to the north. Three companies were inserted on the north side: A/4-39 Inf at 1720 hrs in the center, A/6-31 Inf at 1742 hrs on the west, and C/4-39 Inf at 1912 hrs on the east. At some time during the night all of these companies engaged Viet Cong attempting to escape the encirclement. Because of the great distance between the left and right flanks of the blocking force on the south of the canal, two additional companies were inserted after dark to complete the seal. At 2031 hrs, A/3-39 Inf was placed in the center, to the rear of C/6-31 and A/2-39. Charlie Company, 2-39 Inf, by this time refreshed, was placed at 2100 hrs between B/2-39 Inf on the east and the center.

Sporadic contact continued until 0200 hrs on 12 March. Illumination was provided by Air Force "Spooky" flare ships and artillery. A sweep of the battlefield began at 0400 hrs and the results, coupled with earlier observations, indicated a total enemy body count of seventy-two.

Acts of individual bravery were legion in the contact with an unusually large Viet Cong force. The enemy fire was intense and disciplined. Booby traps and mines made foot movement hazardous, particularly through that part of the battle area which was covered with smoke from the grass fires. Three U.S. soldiers were killed in the action, and twenty more were wounded.

Much later, in mid-April at an evening briefing, the G-2 reported that the 7th ARVN Division had captured a Viet Cong who said his battalion had lost over two hundred men in a battle with the Americans a month earlier. That information was intriguing, and the G-2 was asked to have the POW interrogated to find out more about the contact. The 9th Military Intelligence Unit reported upon interrogation that the contact was with the 261st B Battalion at Thanh Phu on 11 March, and the POW was the equivalent of the battalion adjutant who had made a comprehensive report of the battle to his higher headquarters. This intelligence unit also stated that the POW was a very intelligent, articulate, hardcore Viet Cong, and, upon its ascertaining that the POW had prepared a report of the battle, it was decided to have him recount the battle events. This was the first time the division had ever captured a Viet Cong who could relate in meaningful terms the enemy conduct of a battle. The military intelligence detachment had the prisoner prepare such a report, hoping that we could learn some lessons that would improve our technique and help reduce U.S. casualties. Subsequently, he prepared a detailed account of the Battle of Thanh Phu.

His account was of interest for several reasons. First, although the division had captured many after-action maps sketched by the Viet Cong, it had never obtained a firsthand accounting of enemy actions and tactics during a contact. Second, the detailed reporting provided

Table 15. Box Score, Battle of Thanh Phu

	Reported by United States		Reported by Viet Cong	
Combat statistics	U.S.	VC	U.S.	VC
Forces in combat	630	150–200	1,500	298
Helicopter insertions	101	NA	84	NA
Killed in action	3	72	150	203
Aircraft loss	1	NA	3	NA

Source: Maj. Gen. Harris W. Hollis, "History of the Battle of Thanh Phu, 11–12 March 1969," Headquarters, 9th Infantry Division, Republic of Vietnam, 29 May 1969.

useful insights and lessons learned that could benefit future operations. Third, there was a large disparity of the outcome of the battle between the reports by both combatants.

Because of the POW's detailed reporting, I decided to write an account of the 1st Brigade's participation in the battle for comparative purposes.[1] The parallelism between the two accounts was striking—time of insertions, weapons locations, bunkers, troops maneuvers, all relating very closely. The only major difference was in the box score. When the U.S. statistics are compared to the Viet Cong claims, there are glaring inconsistencies. These, too, tell a story: the conservatism of the U.S. forces versus the exaggerations of the Communists.

According to the POW, the 261th B Battalion had lost 203 KIA during the battle. In addition, about 20 personnel had either deserted or were missing. Finally, most of the battalion's heavy weapons had been lost. As a result of the contact, the battalion was completely ineffective for combat and planned to regroup in Kien Phong Province. Thus, the success of 11 March was even greater than estimated.

Lessons Learned from POW's Account of the Battle of Thanh Phu

As anticipated, several interesting insights about VC procedures and operations were gleaned from the POW's account. (See the full interview in appendix D.) Many reiterated factors we had previously known, but several were new and therefore useful, and these were disseminated to the troops.

VC move their logistical support and their heavy weapons by sampan. When they arrive at a new base area they offload the sampans, set up their weapons, and then camouflage the sampans by sinking them. Quite often variations in the tide will reveal sunken sampans. Sunken sampans can be an indication that a major VC element is in the area. They are a very useful intelligence indicator.

The VC battalions have a central communications center which is normally the battalion headquarters. The battalion headquarters area has a switchboard, radio receivers and transmitters, as well as the message center. During a battle, the VC rely solely upon runners and field phones. They do not use FM radio, for fear of giving their position away. The VC organize their position on the basis of interior lines, and the elimination of a headquarters element would just about remove all possibilities of command and control.

Enemy battalions have a very small highly trained recon element. The 261st B Battalion, for example, had a twelve-man unit. These elements continuously probe our units to find weak spots that the rest of the VC battalion can exploit. The movement and probing of the recon element is continuous; it starts at the advent of a contact and goes on both day and night.

When ordered to withdraw, the VC send out their recon element first. When it has found a route, the heavy weapons company, battalion headquarters, and then the individual elements withdraw, in that order. Consequently, the cessation of mortar and machine-gun fire is an excellent indication that the enemy is withdrawing. Commanders should do everything in their power to attempt to determine the route of withdrawal and block the gap. All VC have been given night training, the most important aspect of which is how to crawl and move at night without being detected. On withdrawals, they mostly move in crouching position. With aerial illumination and observation, as used in the Battle of Thanh Phu, the movements can be detected and effective fire brought to bear.

The VC note the impact area of bombs and artillery, and immediately after impact they move into the craters. The POW stated, "Right after the strikes we would move back into the same area because the U.S. does not bomb into the same area right away." The 9th Division passed this information on to our commanders, and within five days one of the brigades picked up seven body count by clobbering the VC engaged in just that tactic. There are two methods of combating this VC tactic. The preferred method is by having gunships make a pass after every tactical air strike or artillery volley. The other is by having the tactical air and artillery strike the same area twice in a row without any shift.

Interrogation of the VC indicated that his battalion often received advanced warning of planned U.S. troop operations. The battalion commander received the warning message via coded radio transmission. He stated his battalion normally received warning of a planned U.S. operation for the next day the evening before. The 9th Division found the aforementioned to be the case on several occasions. Although it is disconcerting, it shows the requirement for strict security concerning forthcoming operations. It is believed that AO clearance procedures with local Vietnamese authorities led to the leaks. Clearance procedures should be reviewed to preclude such leaks either by the establishment of permanent AOs or by the ability to obtain AOs quickly just prior to an operation.

Defense against CS Gas: The POW said, "The helicopters were dropping the 'crying gas' and a marsh grass fire was set off by smoke grenades. To defend against the gas, we placed a wet cloth across the bunker openings, then lit a candle or burner to cause any gas that might penetrate the bunker to rise to the ceiling while we remained on the floor. This was 100 percent effective. The other method we use is to urinate on a towel and place it over the face. After the attack, we use a 'Chinese Oil' to clear the 'crying gas' from our skin." The 9th Division ran a test on the VC methods and determined that they indeed were effective. However, we found out that during a temperature inversion when the gas persistently stayed on the ground it would penetrate the foxholes. We also found that if we used double doses of gas instead of the normal, single-canister drop the CS would then penetrate the foxholes. A useful technique for friendly troops arises from the foregoing VC tactics. Since the VC stay covered for five to fifteen minutes (the time depending on the persistency of the gas) after a CS attack, then this is a good time for friendly soldiers to maneuver against VC positions.

One of the things that made it difficult for U.S. troops to capture or to have the enemy rally to U.S. forces was the strong rumors spread by the NVA/VC cadres concerning the brutal treatment combatants would receive at the hands of the Americans. (See appendix D for the reflections of Prisoner Phan Xuan Quy, the former battalion secretary of the 261st B Battalion.)

The 1st Brigade continued to wax the enemy. Ambushes and Night Search operations were very successful in interdicting infiltrating VC units. On the night of 20–21 March, gunships of A/7-1 Cavalry, ranging over a wide area during a three-hour Night Search operation, killed thirty VC, most of these infiltrating supplies in small groups. Several days later, on 23 March, a night ambush set near Thanh Hung in southern Base Area 470 trapped the 261st A Battalion, inflicting heavy casualties in the battle.

> The action in Dinh Tuong, on the fringe of Base Area 470, began at about 0400 hours when two companies from the 261 A Viet Cong Main Force Battalion launched an attack against the night ambush positions occupied by two platoons of Company D, 4-39 Inf. The enemy onslaught was supported with heavy fire from rocket launchers and light machine guns. The defenders were not taken by surprise, however. The attackers had been spotted by the alert listening posts as the former had slipped into their attack positions. Thus, the artillery forward observer had called in a fire mission and the ambush patrol leaders had brought their men to a state of complete readiness.
>
> As the Viet Cong approached their positions, men at the listening posts detonated Claymore mines. "They ran into one of our listening posts and got chewed up," said Staff Sergeant Michael Kidd. "Then they backed off and ran into my listening post. We waited until they were nearly on us, then we really shot them up." The exploding Claymores were the signal for the men manning the defensive perimeter to open fire. The enemy advance through the dense undergrowth was riddled with small arms and machine gun fire from the defenders, supplemented by effective artillery rounds. The ensuing enemy flight from the scene was hastened by rocket and minigun fire from 9th Aviation Battalion gunships. Captain Edward Clar, Commander of Company D, declared that the enemy had initiated a planned, coordinated attack, but had completely surrendered the initiative when hit with the mines. "They started yelling and screaming and it gave away their positions."
>
> Just before dawn a sweep of the area was made, revealing thirty-five

bodies and numerous weapons. The Battalion Commander made preparations to pursue the fleeing enemy. Combat tracker dogs were brought in to follow blood trails left by the enemy force, now estimated to be at least two companies. At first light, the infantrymen moved out of their positions and began the chase. Contact was shortly established with a small group, from which a prisoner was taken. Battlefield interrogation by a Tiger Scout disclosed the enemy's withdrawal plan. The tracker dogs and "Recondo" troopers, supported overhead by C/7-1 Cavalry, pursued the enemy relentlessly through the ever-thickening nipa palm. More abandoned equipment and bodies were found. Artillery was repositioned to support the expected contact and additional infantry companies were alerted for a reinforcement mission.

At 1115 hours an aerial observer from the Air Cavalry observed the enemy soldiers moving hurriedly into prepared defensive bunkers. It appeared that the Viet Cong had retreated into their battalion base. Within minutes the Division Forward Air Controller guided Air Force jet strikes onto the bunker complex. Company D, 4-39 Inf, sealed off one side of the position. Companies A and C were inserted by air to the north and south, while A/6-31 Inf was moved in to seal the position on the east. Air strikes and artillery continued to pound the center of the "doughnut."

Eventually the bombs and artillery rounds began to break down the enemy fortifications and many of the enemy soldiers attempted to break and run. One enemy platoon ran headlong into Delta Company, but was unable to breach the encirclement. Other small groups were caught in the open on the south and wiped out by minigun and rocket fire from gunships. By nightfall the seal of the area was complete. Supporting fires poured into the position throughout the night as small bands of Viet Cong tried repeatedly to break out. Company D killed twenty-two of the enemy, defeating five separate escape attempts, and Company A, 4-39 Infantry, killed a like number.

At first light on the 24th, infantrymen moved cautiously into the devastated battle area, but no enemy remained alive to fight. Total body count for the two-day action was 160. In addition, much materiel was captured, including seven machine guns, sixty individual weapons, and parts of mortars, recoilless rifles, radios and other equipment.

The VC Abandon the Winter-Spring Offensive

As seen from the foregoing, in March, the 1st Brigade was having excellent results.

During the same month, the 2nd Brigade was having tremendous success in attriting the enemy in Kien Hoa Province. Utilizing footmobile, airborne, and watermobile assault tactics, it had the Viet Cong on the run, particularly by invading the VC sanctuaries. Captured enemy documents showed the VC political cadre as disturbed that the 2nd Brigade forays into their formerly safe base areas were preventing the VC from attacking Ben Tre, their prime target in Kien Hoa Province. Under Col. Rod Rainville, the 2nd Brigade was making the most of having airmobile assets on a daily basis for the first time, and its three battalions, with skill and daring, were chalking up daily contacts. The Night Search technique, new to the VC in Kien Hoa, was particularly successful in attriting the VC as they attempted to position themselves at night. In March, the 2nd Brigade eliminated 1,185 enemy. The brigade's momentum carried on into April, when they exceeded their March results.[2]

At the same time, the 3rd Brigade was successfully interdicting the enemy as the Viet Cong intensified their efforts to reinforce and resupply their units in Long An Province in preparation for an attack on Saigon. The enemy constantly attempted to push supplies into the area along the major waterways from their sanctuaries in Cambodia. From 14 to 21 March, the 3rd Brigade, in a series of contacts, captured prisoners from eight different VC/NVA units . . . the 267th A, 267th B, 306th, 1st Long An, 2nd Long An, K-4, K-5, and D11 Sapper Battalions. Debriefings of these POWs reaffirmed that the VC units in Long An Province were preparing for an attack on Saigon. Additional intelligence from several sources indicated that the enemy intended a major highpoint near the end of March.

During this three-month period, the division worked hand in glove with RVNAF units. The RF/PF accompanied our teams on MEDCAPs and ICAPs, and teams often spent the night in the hamlets, bolstering the people's sense of security. Fourteen percent of the division's efforts were combined operations with the RVNAF, and the coordination paid off: intelligence was transferred, the enemy was aggressively defeated, and hamlet security was upgraded.

The constant pressure by the 9th Infantry Division and its supporting aviation assets, in coordination with the RVNAF, was steadily taking its toll on the enemy. In March, the 9th Infantry Division operations peaked, eliminating 3,723 enemy. Not only were the Communist troops being heavily attrited, but major caches of weapons and supplies were also being destroyed. The morale of the Viet Cong was rapidly deteriorating, as evidenced by a large increase in the number of senior members of main and local force units rallying to the Vietnamese government. The Communists in the 9th Infantry Division area, for all their efforts in the fourth phase, had not been able to launch a single ground offensive, nor had they managed to create a victory in the thousands of contacts. It was extremely doubtful to us whether the enemy could muster the capability to carry out their planned end-of-March highpoint in our area. This was undoubtedly recognized by the VC/NVA high command, and on 26 March, they terminated their plan for the execution of the Winter-Spring Offensive. The clash of offensives in the Delta had definitely been won overwhelmingly by the Allied Dry Weather Campaign.

To build upon our combat successes, the division published tactical notes, which presented a compendium of tactical innovations that had been successfully used to date. The publication was distributed to all units so as to stimulate commanders to continuously seek new ways of improving the effectiveness of our tactical operations in order to keep a constant pressure on the enemy.[3]

It is difficult to visualize the pace and intensity of the division's operations in the hostile Delta terrain, infested everywhere by mines and booby traps employed by an enemy seriously avoiding contact while attempting to reoutfit, so as to once again take the offensive. During the first three months of 1969, the soldiers of the 9th Division, in more than ten thousand operations, courageously assaulted through the booby traps, located the enemy, and decisively defeated him, eliminating 7,107 combatants in 2,723 contacts while minimizing U.S. casualties (see table 16).

The painstaking work of increasing paddy strength, optimizing aviation assets, integrating intelligence, and developing innovative tactics oriented strictly on the enemy, who was pressured night and day throughout the division area, paid off during the three-month period. Infantry battalions, deployed in company, platoon, and squad-sized units, conducted more than a hundred operations a day, almost half at night, which resulted in thirty contacts per day. Such unrelenting pressure cut off the enemy's infiltration of supplies and replacements,

Table 16. 9th Infantry Division Quarterly Operational Report, January, February, and March 1969

Operations	Contacts	Enemy eliminated	U.S. forces KHA	Enemy eliminated per contact with U.S. forces KHA	U.S. forces KIA per contact	Enemy eliminated per contact
10,551	2,723	7,107	197	36.1	0.07	2.61

Source: Quarterly Operational Reports of 9th Infantry Division, April 1967–June 1969, 9th Infantry Division, Republic of Vietnam.

kept his units off balance, eliminated a great number of combatants, seriously eroded his leadership, and completely thwarted his attack plans. No wonder the Communists called off their vaunted Winter-Spring Offensive.

Unfortunately, these new war-fighting techniques, particularly the aerial night searches and the long-range sniper program, along with the emphasis on night fighting and the increased utilization of air cavalry, made it either very difficult or impossible to retrieve enemy weapons, which, at best, was always hampered by the inundated terrain. In the nine months following the implementation of the constant pressure concept, the division blanketed its area with 26,334 unit combat operations, of which 22,539 made no enemy contact. The fact that 85.5 percent of the unit operations reported no contact belies those detractors who have stated that units received undue pressure to report positive results. It is noteworthy that the 3,795 contacts during the period enabled the division to decimate the enemy in its area.

An Unparalleled and Unequaled Performance

It was understandable, then, that when on 2 April 1969, at the Change of Command ceremony for Maj. Gen. Julian J. Ewell, who was promoted to take over II Field Force Vietnam, that Gen. Creighton Abrams, the MACV commander, told the troops of the 9th Infantry Division, "The performance of this division has been magnificent, and I would say that in the last three months, it's an unparalleled and unequaled performance."

This is the full context of General Abrams's remarks, transcribed from a tape and authenticated by a notary public:

General Ewell, General Hollis, and distinguished visitors, officers and men of the Old Reliables:

I am very happy this morning to have the opportunity to be here with you for a few minutes because I want to pass on to you the high regard with which your performance is regarded by all of us. The performance of this division has been magnificent and I would say that in the last three months, it's an unparalleled and unequaled performance. I think you'll understand that I understand the tremendous part that each and every member of the division has played in this. It's your spirit, your skill and your devotion that has achieved this. But, as everything that is well done, is really done by people and by outstanding people, so it is in this case. General Ewell, your division commander, over a little more than a year has proven to be a brilliant and sensitive commander. His tactical concepts have been characterized by imagination, sensitivity to the kind of situation that you all are in, and he plays hard. General Ewell has been the epitome of the professional soldier—devoted to his country, devoted to his men, and devoted to his profession and the development of it.

Thank you.

Chapter 8

Post–Dong Xuan Operations

The aggressive actions of the RVNAF and the 9th Division in the Delta and U.S. forces and our Allies elsewhere in South Vietnam forced the Communist leaders to abort their Winter-Spring Offensive. Yet, the dispersed and elusive Viet Cong and NVA units that remained in the Upper Delta still had a limited capability to attack population centers and military installations if they were permitted to concentrate forces. We saw how, after the beating they took in the February 1968 Tet Offensive, the Viet Cong were able to mass and attack Saigon again in May. Even after the Mini-Tet losses, they attempted another highpoint in Long An in August and September. Consequently, to prevent yet another Communist attempt at a highpoint and to permit the GVN pacification program to progress, it was necessary for the division to continue to aggressively locate and destroy enemy local and main force units.

Unrelenting Pressure

Maj. Gen. Harris W. Hollis followed Maj. Gen. Julian J. Ewell as the fourth commanding general of the 9th Infantry Division in Vietnam. Under his outstanding leadership, the 9th Division continued to apply unrelenting pressure, night and day, on the enemy. The large Viet Cong losses diluted the Communist leadership, replacements were not as well trained or experienced, the enemy's resupply of weapons and ammunition was being interdicted and the people rallying to the GVN reduced his food supply. As the Viet Cong capabilities weakened, ours strengthened. In April and May, the 9th Division continued to operate full-bore and eliminated more than six thousand enemy (see table 14). The net result was that the Viet Cong Infrastructure eroded and pacification greatly improved. During April and May, seven different main

Table 17. Major Unit Contacts, April and May 1969

Date	Enemy unit	Enemy losses
8 April	K-4 Battalion	42 NVA KIA
18 April	K-5 Battalion	31 NVA KIA
26 April	K-6 Battalion	63 NVA KIA
10 May	580th Battalion	49 VC KIA
13 May	267th Battalion	83 VC KIA
14 May	K-4 Battalion	30 NCA KIA
22 May	261th Artillery	105 VC KIA
24 May	516th Battalion	90 VC KIA

Source: 9th Infantry Division field reports, April and May 1969.

force Viet Cong and NVA units were tracked down, surrounded, and defeated, keeping the enemy off balance and denying him any offensive capabilities.[1]

These large battles were very important in preempting the Communist offensive operations by destroying and capturing the enemy. However, the pay-off was the result of unprecedented thousands of small-unit operations applying constant pressure, causing the Viet Cong structure to fall apart. The Communists lost their leaders, their followers, their weapons and ammunition, and their food. They were ineffective and on the run, unable to mount an offensive. The dedication and bravery of all the 9th Division soldiers was the key to this success.

The torrid pace of the offensive operations went on, insuring a constant twenty-four-hour pressure on the enemy. From 27 March to 26 April 1969, over 3,000 VC were eliminated, about three per contact (see table 18). In our efforts to cover the large tactical area in order to interdict the enemy, there were 2,452 operations where no contact was made. However, those operations often paid off in other ways, such as enabling units like the 3rd Brigade to discover enemy caches.

> While conducting operations, the men of the 3rd Brigade uncovered a huge enemy cache containing 128 60 mm mortar rounds, 37,000 AK-47 rounds, fifty boxes of 60mm fuses, fifty-two cans of 60mm charges, thirty-eight anti-tank grenades, and 296 82 mm mortar rounds.

Table 18. 9th Infantry Division operations, 27 March–26 April 1969

Operations	Squad	Platoon	Company	Total
Day	15/8	865/76	569/631	1,449/715
Night	1,075/155	691/121	357/129	2,123/405
Total	1,090/163	1,556/197	926/760	3,572/1,120

Source: Maj. Gen. Harris W. Hollis, Letter to Commanding General, II Field Force, Vietnam, APO 96266, Subject: Recommendation for Award of the Presidential Unit Citation, Headquarters, 9th Infantry Division, Republic of Vietnam, May 1969.

During the first five months of 1969, the 9th Division, in coordination with its Vietnamese allies, preempted all efforts by the Communists to implement their Winter-Spring Offensive, requiring them to abort their plans. During the five-month period, the division eliminated 13,264 enemy, of which 4,604 were the result of highly successful night operations, which restricted the Viet Cong's ability to move under the cover of darkness (see table 14). Within that number, 539 POWs were captured, 249 Hoi Chanhs rallied to U.S. troops, and 87 members of the Viet Cong infrastructure were held as civil defendants. Additionally, 3,030 Viet Cong within the division area rallied to the GVN, undoubtedly as the result of the constant pressure of the 9th Division and its RVNAF allies.

The techniques and tactics of the superb unit commanders and the indomitable spirit of the infantry and airmen raised the effectiveness of combat operations to an all-time high, and during this period the elimination ratio was 44 to 1. As the result of improved tactics and techniques, U.S. casualties were kept to the minimum possible. Even so, 301 brave soldiers were killed in action, and 3,512 were wounded, a heavy sacrifice.

The division did everything possible to train and to provide necessary support for our soldiers to ensure their safety. However, should a soldier be wounded, the unit medics were there to treat him as soon as possible; and if the wounds were serious a dust-off helicopter was always on call to effect a medical evacuation to the nearest hospital. Dedicated combat medics supported by on-call medical evacuation helicopters saved the lives of many wounded soldiers.

Fig. 20. A combat casualty

Specialist Richard Montro, a combat medic with Company D. 2-39 Inf, distinguished himself by his gallant actions with the 1st Brigade during an enemy contact in Cai Be District of Dinh Tuong Province. While sweeping through dense vegetation, Montro's company found themselves in the middle of a heavily booby trapped area. Two men were wounded by booby traps and the medic crawled fifty meters under enemy sniper fire to treat them. When the wounded had been evacuated to a pick up zone for dust-off, fire, Montro exposed himself countless times while running across the open paddies to treat the wounded. When the medical evacuation helicopter arrived again, the medic stood up to direct the ship to a landing. This selfless devotion to duty under adverse conditions has become the key to the spirit of the 9th Division soldier in searching out and engaging a tough enemy in his treacherous lair.

Chapter 9

Pacification Results

The endgame was pacification, and the success of the 9th Division can be measured by not only its combat results but also the improvements of the GVN pacification program. Of great importance was that the GVN won the "rice war." The improved security prevented the Viet Cong from appropriating appreciable supplies, and, after the major disruption of the Communist General Offensive in 1968, agricultural production improved from a low point of 84 percent of the index based upon the 1961–1965 period to 94 percent in 1969 and 103 percent in 1970. The rice output in the Delta continued to grow, and in 1973 agricultural production was 115 percent of what it had been in the base period.[1]

It was heartening to see heavy traffic on the main routes and farmers' vehicles carrying squeaking pigs and squawking chickens on the secondary roads where just a year previously nothing traveled because of VC interdictions. Unquestionably, the economy of the Delta was improving greatly.

Probably the best way to measure pacification progress is to view the results of the Hamlet Evaluation Surveys in the 9th Division's tactical area of responsibility, which, commencing in June 1968, included the four Northern Delta provinces of Long An, Dinh Tuong, Kien Hoa, and Go Cong. The VC/NVA initiated their General Offensive and General Uprising campaign to rally the South Vietnamese population to the Communist side. As is shown in table 8, in the 9th Division TAOR, even after his first two major offenses, the enemy had failed to increase population control. In June 1968, the division had consolidated at Dong Tam, divested itself of most static missions, established fire support bases in the heart of VC territory, and implemented its new tactical concepts. Subsequently, its tactical successes decimated

Table 19. Viet Cong Population Control,
Hamlet Evaluation Survey, "V" Rated

Province	Hamlets		Population	
	13 January 1968	31 July 1969	31 January 1968	13 July 1969
Dinh Tuong	350	192	230,642	120,251
Kien Hoa	352	82	258,830	71,851
Go Cong	77	15	40,210	1,278
Long An	282	109	132,268	45,700
Total	1,061	398	661,950	239,080

Source: Hamlet Evaluation Survey

the VC/NVA main and local force units, thereby allowing the GVN process of pacification to accelerate. Consequently, the VC lost control of much of the Upper Delta's population. Over 420,000 people were freed from VC control (see table 19). Prior to the 1968 Tet Offensive, the VC controlled 62 percent (1,061) of the 1,720 hamlets in the area. By the end of July 1969, when the division rotated home, 23 percent (398) were still under VC control, and that number was diminishing rapidly.

Reviewing the other side of the ledger, in this same period GVN control of hamlets increased from 179 to 408, and the population under GVN influence increased by more than 410,000 people. The results could have been even greater, because with the rapid expansion of the GVN into the less secure areas of the countryside, the civil services of the government were unable to keep pace with the gains made by the combined U.S. and Vietnamese military forces.

At the time the loss of control of over 660 hamlets and 420,000 inhabitants resulted in irreparable damage to VC efforts; the VC were no longer able to impress young men or to have the villagers prepare positions or carry supplies. More important, the VC capabilities to commandeer rice and other essential items necessary to support their guerrilla activities were greatly reduced. As a consequence, the fourth phase of the Communists' General Offensive and General Uprising collapsed and was a dismal failure.

Notwithstanding this outstanding success, the tug-of-war was still ongoing in the contested hamlets, where several hundred thousand people lived. However, now that the VC/NVA main and local force units had been severely mauled, the GVN continued successfully to pacify the countryside so that by the end of 1972, there were no VC controlled hamlets in the Upper Delta.

Despite the great success of the division's pacification efforts, there were some who decried the collateral damage resulting from military operations. If one considers that the 9th Division was required to evict the VC from the major urban areas of Saigon—My Tho, Can Tho, and Ben Tre, to name a few—where fierce house-to-house fighting occurred, then collateral damage was to be expected. One correspondent bemoaned that the tranquility of the peasants living in VC base areas was disturbed by attacks, not considering that these areas furnished the sustenance and manpower to the VC units terrorizing the GVN-controlled hamlets and urban centers. In the populated Delta area, where it was often extremely difficult to differentiate friend from foe, there was always an opportunity for collateral damage, particularly when one of the VC tactics was to fire upon Allied Forces from built-up areas. Unquestionably, sometimes noncombatants unfortunately were harmed. To ensure that such incidents were kept to the minimum, the division had strict rules of engagement; for example, no artillery fire was allowed within one kilometer of a hamlet. The enemy situation required that the division conduct many small-unit operations at night to cover such a large area as to interdict the movements of enemy personnel and equipment. Table 18 shows that there were 3,572 operations in just one month, of which 30 percent were squad-sized and 60 percent were at night. With such intense operations, civilian casualties sometimes occurred. Whenever injuries came to our attention, solatium was instantly offered. The division was vitally interested in building up its area, not tearing it down. The GVN fully understood this. Although, regrettably, there were some civilian casualties, over 420,000 people were liberated from VC control.

GVN Recognition of the 9th Infantry Division

In early June 1969, Gen. Cao Van Vien, the chairman of the Vietnamese Joint General Staff, journeyed to Dong Tam to present the members of the 9th Division with its second Vietnamese Presidential Cross of Gallantry, in recognition of its magnificent combat record, and at the same time he also awarded the division, on behalf of a grateful GVN, the Civil Action Honor Medal, First Class for significant services in the common struggle against Communism. The citation reads:

> Serving in Vietnam from 19 December 1966 to the present, the 9th United States Infantry Division has obtained many significant results in the spheres of Warfare and Civic Actions. Especially in the area of Civic Actions, the 9th United States Infantry Division's soldiers, in spite of hardship, carried out their activities in remote hamlets in helping the Vietnamese people through their medical support, education and psychological warfare assistance, repair and construction of public facilities for the war victims. In the area of public health, the 9th United States Infantry Division has trained 158 Public Health Cadres, given medical examinations and treated 708,588 persons. In the educational domain, the 9th United States Infantry Division constructed and equipped 356 Schools in Tien Giang; Dong Tam and My Tho areas. In the psychological warfare area, the 9th United States Infantry Division has carried out a good deal of loudspeaker and leaflet dropping missions, resulting in 8,949 Viet Cong Cadres surrendering. In addition, the 9th United States Infantry Division provided 48,256 manpower hours to help local people in repairing the destroyed houses; furnished 89 Orphanages with construction materials; distributed 1,000 tons of food and 8 tons of clothes to refugees of the Communist aggression. Through the above achievements, the 9th United States Infantry Division has contributed greatly to the common struggle against Communism, as well as helped the Republic of Vietnam in its reconstruction.[2]

This was the *first time ever* that a military unit had been awarded the Vietnamese Civil Action Medal. It was remarkable that the 9th Division received an award from the Vietnamese people for humanitarian actions while at the same time being cited for gallantry in inflicting over ten thousand casualties on the enemy over a five-month period. The Vietnamese government gratefully acknowledged 9th Division's integrated approach to combat operations and pacification.

Communist Assessment of Delta Pacification

According to the Hamlet Evaluation System, during 1968 and 1969 in the IV Corps area, the Communists lost control of over 1 million persons; this did not go unnoticed by the North Vietnamese.

Fig. 21. An afternoon stroll with local orphans

In late 1973, the RVNAF JGS J-2 produced a study, "Communists' Assessment of the RVNAF." In wartime, it is always important to know the enemy, and the NVA perceptions of the RVNAF were crucial intelligence that helped the RVNAF to understand enemy tactics. The J-2 Study relied primarily upon official enemy reports or assessment records on the spirit and combat capabilities of the RVNAF which were published by Communist technical agencies and which were very difficult to acquire because of their high classification of VN

ABSOLUTE SECRET. The North Vietnamese perceived the struggle in South Vietnam as being conducted in phases. The fifth period, 1967–1969, was called The Implementation of the General Offensive and Uprising phase. As mentioned previously, one of the main Communist goals was to defeat the GVN pacification program, thereby maintaining control of the manpower and economic resources of the countryside. The NVN classified documents specifically mentioned the GVN success in pacifying the Mekong Delta. The summary of the J-2 study for the 1967–1969 period is quoted in full here.

> 5. *Period 1967–1969* (Implementation of the general offensive and uprising phase).
>
> Communist General Offensive Phases 1 and 2 against SVN cities were abortive. The Communists Party Central Committee assessed that they committed an error in strategy for having launched the abortive offensive without careful preparations. On the other hand, the timely counteroffensive of RVNAF foiled their plan and the RVNAF was able to firmly hold its areas of control. On the contrary, the Communist infrastructures and local forces were destroyed. Communist documents and ranking cadre admitted that the RVNAF was able to stabilize its fighting spirit and its sense of responsibility for national defense.[3]
>
> In mid-1969, the RVNAF was widely deployed throughout the rural areas and encroached upon all areas temporarily controlled by the Communists. *The RVNAF was very successful in the pacification of the Mekong Delta.* Furthermore, the Communists recognized the pacification successes attained by the RVNAF throughout SVN and confessed that they sustained heavy losses during the two phases of the 1968 Offensive Drive.

Chapter 10

A Total Division Effort

This discussion has focused primarily on the combat capabilities of infantrymen and their direct support organizations: the artillery, air cavalry, assault helicopters, Air Force, and Navy. Many other units not specifically mentioned—such as the 45th Infantry Platoon (Scout Dog), the 65th Infantry Platoon (Combat Tracker), the Air Cushion Vehicle Platoon, the 1097th Transportation Company (Medium Boat), and the 15th Engineer Combat Battalion—also participated in ferreting out and destroying the enemy.

> For example, on 26 April, while en route to conduct a cordon and search operation, B/2-47 Infantry received very heavy fire from a large enemy unit which was fortified in bunkers. The company occupied a blocking position while air strikes and artillery were brought to bear on the enemy until they could be reinforced by other units. When the reinforcement arrived, which were C/2-47 Infantry and two platoons of D Company, 15th Engineer Battalion, the assault was renewed. Sixty-three enemy of the K-6 Battalion, 1st NVA Regiment were killed.

Yet, all units of the division contributed to its combat success. The importance of the medical battalion needs no explanation. Not only did the doctors, nurses, and corpsmen maintain the health of the troops, but they were instrumental in the humanitarian efforts on behalf of the Vietnamese people, thus fostering pacification. The 9th Signal Battalion provided outstanding communications, so essential to combat effectiveness. The aircraft and other equipment were maintained and repaired by the 709th Maintenance Battalion. Its mechanics were often called upon at night to fly over enemy territory to repair radars. The 9th Supply and Transportation Battalion kept an average of thirty-eight trucks per day on the roads to supply the brigades, traveling over roads that were mined and subject to ambushes. They also operated aircraft rearm and refuel points in forward areas under hazardous conditions. The finance, judge advocate, and adjutant general units formed contact teams that spent days at a time with infantry battalions at base camps to review finance records, pay troops, and provide personal and legal advice to ensure that the morale of the troops was kept high. All of the division's soldiers were constantly in harm's way because of the constant Viet Cong mortar attacks.

> Early in the morning of 26 March 1969, "Old Reliables" living in the Dong Tam base camp were roused out of bed by one more of the frequent enemy mortar attacks. This one took a very serious turn when a mortar touched off a tremendous explosion in the base ammunition dump. The explosion, which shook buildings as much as a mile and a half away, destroyed close to 500 tons of ammunition, and caused fifty-eight casualties, most of whom were Navy personnel living near the dump.

As another example, the MASH hospital at Dong Tam had inflatable buildings. During an enemy attack by fire, mortar fragments would often perforate the buildings, creating serious problems for the hospital staff who were treating patients. So concrete walls were built for protection; ultimately, key hospital locations, such as the operating rooms, had to be almost totally encased in concrete for the wonderful medical personnel to be able to treat the troops safely and without interruption from VC attacks by fire.

Clerks, cooks, mechanics, and others constantly manned the base-camp perimeters and were subject to direct fire attacks by the enemy on many occasions.

> While repulsing an enemy mortar and rocket attack on the Brigade Headquarters at Tan An, Sergeant First Class Robert F. Baugher demonstrated that feats of heroism are not confined to the rice paddies, but that support troops, too, are capable of valor in the face of the enemy. Baugher, on perimeter guard at Tan An, was one of the first to react to enemy movement spotted outside the berm. When his section of the perimeter received enemy rockets from close range, he went from bunker to bunker encouraging his men, redistributing ammunition, and removing the wounded. He

Fig. 22. A church service

personally defended a bunker that had received two hits from the rockets and kept the enemy from penetrating his defense.

The examples of individual bravery beyond the call of duty are virtually legion . . . a daily thing expected as a matter of course from not only the infantrymen but the helicopter pilots, the artillerymen in far-flung fire support bases, and even the cooks and clerks manning the defensive perimeters.

The unflinching dedication to duty and the outstanding performance of all the brave men and women of the 9th Infantry Division and its supporting units in Vietnam contributed to its unsurpassed combat record from February 1967 through July 1969.

Chapter 11

The Division Rotates Home

In June, the 9th Division received word that it was to rotate to the United States, and units began to prepare to stand down. The 2nd Brigade terminated operations on 4 July; the 1st Brigade on 23 July; and on 26 July, the 3rd Brigade went under operational control of II Field Force, Vietnam.

From its entry into the Mekong Delta in February 1967 until July 1969, the 9th Infantry Division had been an effective fighting unit developing tactics and techniques, from riverine to Night Search operations, to meet the ever-changing Viet Cong and NVA initiatives. The 9th Division soldiers in this period distinguished themselves by their outstanding performance of duty and their extraordinary heroism in action against enemy forces. Operating by air, water, and land, they successfully overcame the extremely hazardous and difficult Delta terrain and inflicted defeat after defeat upon an elusive enemy, substantially advancing the cause of pacification. A review of the 9th Division's operations in this thirty-month period, which were directed toward improving the security of the Delta and enhancing the GVN's pacification program, is in order.

Initially, the aggressiveness of the division, the first and only American combat infantry units to operate in the densely populated Delta, surprised the enemy. In 1967 the riverine brigade ranged far and wide on the Delta's waterways—attacking the enemy, which was ill prepared to defend against riverine tactics—and the 1st Brigade policed the vital People's Road and its surrounding territory, inflicting substantial losses on the VC.

Notwithstanding their losses, the VC were able to fully reconstitute their units in preparation for the first phase of North Vietnam's General Offensive and General Uprising Campaign, which began on

31 January 1968, the day of the important Tet national holiday. This was a major COSVN offensive, and the VC attacked and temporarily occupied parts of Saigon and all the major cities of the Delta. The division's versatile tactical mobility allowed it to move expeditiously to the besieged areas by road, air, and water and forcibly root out the enemy which suffered serious losses, particularly among the previously hidden VC infrastructure, whose members had to surface in order to support the attacks. The Tet Offensive was a failure in that the VC gained no territory and there had been no uprising by the Vietnamese people in the Delta. However, the North Vietnamese gained great cachet in the world press.

The Communists, buoyed by the spin on their Tet Offensive, decided to quickly reconstitute their forces and to strike again at Saigon from its vulnerable southern area. Although in the three months succeeding Tet the VC were unable to fully reconstitute their units, they nevertheless massed again for an attack on Saigon in early May 1968. This second phase of the "General Offensive" (Mini-Tet) was also a complete failure. The division's 3rd Brigade successfully contained the attack so not a single VC unit reached Saigon proper. The Communists' Central Committee assessed phases 1 and 2 and found they were abortive and that they had committed an error in strategy.[1] VC losses were substantial in these two offenses, and they had not only not gained any additional control of the population but they had managed to alienate the Vietnamese so that the people wanted to be able to better protect themselves. Thus the concept of the People Self Defense Force (PSDF) was initiated. The end of May 1968 was the apogee of Communist influence in the Delta; from here on out the Communists began to lose the tug-of-war for population control. Again the VC retreated to their base areas.

By the summer, the division was becoming much more effective in rooting out VC units located in their previously sacrosanct base areas. COSVN, with its credo of the offensive, was not to be deterred, and it again planned to attack Saigon from the south in the early fall. The 1st Brigade, utilizing jitterbugging and seal-and-pile-on tactics, crushed the enemy's third offensive, again inflicting serious losses. The tide had definitely turned in the war in the Upper Delta. Not only was the enemy on the run, but the GVN had greatly expanded and upgraded its Regional and Popular Forces. The PSDF had grown rapidly in 1968 and 1969 to over a million trained personnel. These RF, PF, and PSDF units brought security to the local population once the Viet Cong main force units had been neutralized, which was the responsibility of the ARVN and U.S. troops. At year's end, the GVN was positioned to fully support pacification.

COSVN initiated a fourth phase of the general offensive, the Winter-Spring Offensive, in early 1969, whose purpose was among other items "to liberate the rural areas and attack enemy lines of communication." This time, their offensive coincided with the IV Corp Tactical Zone Dry Weather Campaign, which fortuitously provided the division with appreciably more vital nonorganic aircraft. Not only that, but the division had perfected its sniper program and the Night Search techniques, which enabled us to take the night from the enemy, thereby seriously suppressing his movements to reposition men and material. The enemy suffered defeat after defeat in a continuing series of battles as he attempted to position himself for major attacks. During the Dry Weather Campaign, the division concentrated on supporting GVN pacification efforts and was able to upgrade 217 out of 243 GVN-targeted hamlets, a superb record.

By early spring, the VC units were completely beaten up, and as their capabilities flagged many VC rallied to the Allied Forces. Enemy recruiting was at its lowest point, and the Central Committee was for the first time required to send major NVA units into the Delta to support the unraveling VC. The 9th Division swiftly defeated these units. The vastly improved security in the Upper Delta enabled the civil services of the GVN pacification program to become effective, and the local population under GVN control increased by more than 410,000 people. Rice production increased, and the farm-to-market roads were opened and safe to all traffic.

The statistical results of the division's two and a half years of combat operations are shown in table 20.[2] Overall, 34,044 enemy were eliminated. This might seem a large number, but when one adds up all of the main and local forces, guerrillas, VCI personnel, casualties, constant requirement for replacements, and transient resupply personnel, the greater than 50 percent attrition rate is reasonable, particularly when the RVNAF forces in 1973–1974, without the powerful U.S. ground and air support, attrited 24 percent of the NVA/VC combat personnel.[3]

Success was not without sacrifice and a heavy cost in battlefield casualties—1,869 brave soldiers were killed in hostile action, and 16,232 were wounded.

The net effect of the division's operations was that the Viet Cong structure in the Upper Delta was devastated—the Communists lost thousands of combatants, their weapons and ammunition, and their access to the resources of the rice-rich Delta. Substantial losses were sustained by the guerrilla forces, which made it very difficult for the Main Force/Local Force units to be supported and maintained. Enemy units were on the run and in hiding and were ineffective. They were permanently unable to reconstitute their formerly coercive presence, as evidenced by the extraordinary fact that, according to the January 1973 U.S.-supervised Hamlet Evaluation Survey, not one of the 1,720 hamlets in the Upper Delta Provinces of Long An, Dinh Tuong, Go Cong, and Kien Hoa was rated as being under VC control (a V rating) and 93.4 percent of the 1,749,444 people were living under GVN control (an A, B, or C rating).

Not only were the Viet Cong units in the Delta decimated, but the Allied Forces throughout South Vietnam had decisively defeated the NVA/VC units elsewhere in 1967–1969, particularly during the abortive Communist General Offensive and General Uprising. It has been estimated that in these three years, the Communists lost 545,000 personnel.[4] The ranks of the VC had been greatly reduced, and the conflict from 1970 onward was a NVA war, carried out by men and materiel from North Vietnam. By the war's end, 80 percent of combatants were NVA. In the six years from the 1 January 1967 major American build-up until our departure in January 1973, the valiant Allied Forces eliminated almost 1 million NVA/VC in thousands of actions throughout South Vietnam.[5]

During the Vietnam War, the Delta was always a primary battleground of NVA/VC operations, since the Communist objectives were to conquer people and territory and the Delta had the most arable land and population. From 1973 to 1975, after the U.S. withdrawal from South Vietnam, there were by far more incidents, more major battles, more RVNAF killed and wounded, and more enemy killed in Military Region IV than in any other military region. A major conflict was continuously waged in the Delta, unfortunately off the radar screen of many observers.[6]

The 9th Division was the only major U.S. unit operating south of Saigon and we coordinated with all levels of the GVN, from the joint general staff to the smallest district organization, particularly with respect to exchanging intelligence information. We conducted joint operations with the ARVN and trained many units in sniper techniques and ground and air operations. The division conducted numerous civic actions in support of the GVN pacification program. A grateful GVN awarded the division its highest honors, for valor in recognition of its total dominance of an elusive enemy, and the Civic Action Medal, for its humanitarian support of the Vietnamese people.

The 9th Infantry Division's mission when it was introduced into the Delta was to deny the Communists access to the resources of the region and to improve security, to make possible the political and social aspects of the GVN's pacification program. That mission was accomplished.

Years later, on 1 July 1991, Gen. W. C. Westmoreland wrote in a letter to General Sullivan, the current Department of the Army chief of staff, "What sets the record of the Ninth apart is that they not only totally dominated the enemy, but they did it over a period of months—an unheard of feat of arms."[7]

Table 20. 9th Infantry Division Statistical Results, February 1967–July 1969

	Enemy KIA	POWs	Hoi Chanh	VCI	Total losses	U.S. KHA	U.S. WHA	Total casualties	Enemy KIA versus U.S. KHA	Total enemy losses versus total U.S. casualties
1967										
February	66	13	–	–	79	–	–	–	–	–
March	471	28	–	–	499	33	260	291	14.3:1	1.70:1
April	751	61	–	–	812	33	260	293	22.8:1	2.77:1
May	533	38	–	–	571	33	516	549	16.2:1	1.04:1
June	590	25	–	–	615	55	366	421	10.7:1	1.46:1
July	636	117	–	–	753	43	324	367	14.8:1	2.05:1
August	278	99	–	–	377	27	279	306	10.3:1	1.23:1
September	418	56	–	–	474	45	382	427	9.3:1	1.11:1
October	262	29	–	–	291	26	218	344	10.1:1	0.85:1
November	269	24	–	–	293	50	463	513	5.4:1	0.57:1
December	578	44	1	–	623	50	506	556	22.6:1	1.12:1
1968										
January	594	87	–	–	681	96	697	793	6.2:1	0.86:1
February	1,872	51	1	–	1,924	146	1,261	1,407	12.8:1	1.37:1
March	665	53	2	–	731	42	714	756	15.8:1	0.97:1
April	671	101	5	–	777	108	558	666	6.2:1	1.17:1
May	1,554	113	1	–	1,668	113	881	994	13.8:1	1.68:1

Table 20. 9th Infantry Division Statistical Results, February 1967–July 1969 (cont'd)

	Enemy KIA	POWs	Hoi Chanh	VCI	Total losses	U.S. KHA	U.S. WHA	Total casualties	Enemy KIA versus U.S. KHA	Total enemy losses versus total U.S. casualties
June	888	69	7	–	964	113	522	635	7.9:1	1.52:1
July	646	84	5	–	735	54	394	448	12.0:1	1.64:1
August	968	108	9	–	1,085	101	549	650	9.6:1	1.67:1
September	735	104	12	–	851	67	547	614	11.0:1	1.39:1
October	901	92	25	–	1,018	66	378	444	13.7:1	2.29:1
November	961	140	22	–	1,123	44	360	404	21.9:1	2.78:1
December	968	101	26	13	1,108	59	519	578	16.4:1	1.92:1
1969										
January	1,292	95	24	24	1,435	92	636	728	14.0:1	1.9:1
February	1,799	82	42	26	1,949	59	626	685	30.0:1	2.8:1
March	3,504	124	75	20	3,723	46	822	868	76.0:1	4.3:1
April	3,117	116	71	6	3,310	39	630	669	80.0:1	4.9:1
May	2,677	122	37	11	2,847	65	798	863	41.0:1	3.3:1
June	1,792	127	55	7	1,981	45	614	659	40.0:1	3.0:1
July	680	49	18	0	747	19	272	291	36.0:1	2.6:1
Total	31,136	2,363	438	107	34,044	1,869	16,232	18,101	16.7:1	1.9:1

Appendix A
9th Infantry Division and Assigned and Attached Units, 1969

Headquarters and Headquarters Company, 9th Infantry Division
Headquarters and Headquarters Company, 1st Brigade
Headquarters and Headquarters Company, 2nd Brigade
Headquarters and Headquarters Company, 3rd Brigade
6th Battalion, 31st Infantry
2nd Battalion, 39th Infantry
3rd Battalion, 39th Infantry
4th Battalion, 39th Infantry
2nd Battalion, 47th Infantry
3rd Battalion, 47th Infantry
4th Battalion, 47th Infantry
2nd Battalion, 47th Infantry
3rd Battalion, 47th Infantry
5th Battalion, 60th Infantry
Headquarters and Headquarters Battery, 9th Infantry Division Artillery
  2nd Battalion, 4th Artillery
  1st Battalion, 11th Artillery
  3rd Battalion, 34th Artillery
  2nd Battalion, 84th Artillery
  Battery C, 5th Battalion (AW) (SP), 2nd Artillery
  2nd Platoon, Battery H (Searchlight), 29th Artillery
9th Aviation Battalion
D Troop, 3rd Squadron, 5th Cavalry
Headquarters and Headquarters Company, 214th Combat Aviation Battalion
  162nd Assault Helicopter Company
  191st Assault Helicopter Company

240th Assault Helicopter Company
A Troop, 7th Squadron, 1st Cavalry
C Troop, 7th Squadron, 1st Cavalry
A Troop, 3rd Squadron, 17th Cavalry
B Troop, 3rd Squadron, 17th Cavalry
Headquarters and Headquarters Company and Band, 9th Infantry Division
Support Command
  9th Administration Company
  9th Medical Battalion
  9th Supply and Transport Battalion
  709th Maintenance Battalion
  1097th Transportation Company (Medium Boat)
15th Engineer Battalion
9th Signal Battalion
9th Military Police Company
Company E (Ranger), 75th Infantry
335th Radio Research Company
43rd Infantry Platoon (Scout Dog)
45th Infantry Platoon (Scout Dog)
65th Infantry Platoon (Combat Tracker)
Armor Platoon, Air Cushion Vehicle
9th Military Intelligence Detachment
584th Military Intelligence Detachment
39th Chemical Detachment
19th Military History Detachment
18th Public Information Detachment
19th Public Information Detachment
22nd Public Information Detachment
361st Aviation Detachment (Divisional), 165th Aviation Group (Cbt)
9th Infantry Division Detachment, United States Army Special Security Group
OL5, 5th Weather Squadron (USAF)
9th Infantry Division Tactical Air Control Party, 19th Tactical Air Support Squadron (USAF)
14th Military Intelligence Detachment (ARVN)

Appendix B
9th Infantry Division Task Organization, January–April 1969

Headquarters and Headquarters Company, 9th Infantry Division

1st Brigade	2nd Brigade	3rd Brigade
6/31st Infantry	3/47th Infantry	2/47th Infantry (M)
2/39th Infantry	4/47th Infantry	2/60th Infantry
3/39th Infantry	3/60th Infantry	5/60th Infantry
4/39th Infantry	3/34th Artillery (DS)*	2/4th Artillery (DS)
1/11th Artillery (DS)	1097th Trans Co (Medium Boat) (DS)	C/15th Engineer (DS)
A/15th Engineer (DS)	D/15th Engineer (DS)	240th Assault Helicopter Company (DS)
191st Assault Helicopter Company (DS)	162nd Assault Helicopter Company (DS)	A/3/17th Cavalry (DS)**
B/3/17th Cavalry (DS)**	D/3/5th Cavalry (DS)	B/3/17th Cavalry (DS) **
A/7/1st Cavalry (DS)**	C/7/1st Cavalry (DS)**	

General Support Troops

Division Artillery	Support Command	Division Troops

Notes: * Direct Support
** Periodic Assignment

Appendix C
The Story of a Booby-Trap Casualty

The battalion has the assault helicopter assets today and members of the 2nd Platoon Alpha Company are on the PZ waiting for the "slicks." Amongst the 2nd Squad is PFC Jones, infantryman, in-country for six weeks. The assault helicopters arrive and the 2nd Platoon fills five slicks. As they lift off the PZ, the day's reconnaissance in force has started. About 20 minutes later, the 30 combat infantrymen are inserted 300 meters from a nipa line along a canal on the edge of the Plain of Reeds. Upon insertion, the men hit the ground behind a paddy dike, but it is a cold LZ. The platoon leader is now issuing instructions to move to the north and check the nipa line. It is about 1100 hrs in the morning as the men are closing in toward some dense underbrush in the tall coconut trees. So far, there has been no fire, however, they can see bunkers interspersed amongst the edge of the foliage. The Tiger Scout who is walking point raises his hand, indicating something suspicious. Everyone halts, and the squad leader comes forward to see what's up. A visual inspection indicates a trip-wire grenade booby trap carefully camouflaged amongst the foliage.

> (The majority of all booby traps are detected in the early morning, when troops are fresh. Many of the booby traps are detected by the several hundred Tiger Scouts, former VC themselves with an intimate knowledge of VC tactics and techniques, which the 9th Infantry Division has operating with the troops in the field. 70% of all booby traps encountered are detected. 72% are trip-wire grenade types. 36% of all booby traps encountered are in the jungle. Only 6% of these booby traps are covered by VC fire; that is, 94% have no one covering them, or if the VC are covering them, they don't fire. The majority of all grenade booby traps are Chicom.)

Having seen that the pin is still in the Chicom grenade, the squad leader instructs the Tiger Scout to cut the trip-wire, rendering the grenade safe. This having been done, they destroy the grenade and the platoon moves forward again and, encountering no more booby traps, they check the bunkers. Finding no VC, they blow the biggest bunkers and return to the rice paddies and a new PZ, ready for pickup and additional airmobile insertions elsewhere.

Two more insertions follow, one of which results in an enemy contact. The troops are proud of their two VC body count and the one AK-47 captured. Towards the end of the day, at 1600 hrs, they are inserted again, this time approximately 300 meters from another nipa line along another canal where intelligence has indicated there may be VC. Again, they are instructed to move out and check the nipa for VC activity. By now, the point man has changed three times, and PFC Jones is walking point. He is tired. Although during the dry season there is not any water in the rice paddies, Jones nevertheless is walking along the rice paddy dike where the movement is quicker, because during the dry season the paddies are broken and the footing is difficult. His buddies are in the same frame of mind and instead of walking as skirmishers, they follow a single line. They are bunched up, too, as they move forward. They really don't expect anything and everyone is as relaxed as you can get in the rice paddies . . . which isn't very relaxed. About 100 meters from the nipa line, Jones hears a POP. He realizes that he has set off a booby trap. But Jones freezes, he can't move, he can't speak. The booby trap goes off and Jones and two buddies just behind him are hit by fragments.

> (The 9th Division statistics show that 40 percent of all casualties occur to soldiers in-country less than two months. 30 percent of all booby traps encountered during the month of April were inadvertently detonated. 34 percent of all booby traps found were on trails and rice paddy dikes. 16 percent of these booby traps were pressure type. 36 percent were buried in the ground.)

Jones has been seriously wounded. His foot is torn up; he has fragments in the gut. God! How it hurts! Dustoff is called immediately and it arrives 20 minutes later, taking Jones and his two buddies to the hospital at Dong Tam. One of his buddies is lucky. He is treated and released. Jones is sent immediately to the operating room.

> (During the month of April, 75 percent of all men wounded by booby traps were hospitalized. 46 percent of all the detonated booby traps resulted in multiple casualties. An average of 2.9 men were wounded per multiple incident.)

Jones, back from the operating room, has had a lot of time to think it over. The doctors hope to save his foot, but right now he is awfully glad just to be alive. He relives that terrible moment in the paddy dike. But he was tired, and he was not paying attention to where he put his feet. Brown, the other man hospitalized, a veteran of eight months in the paddies, knows he should not have been walking so close to the point man. However, the detonation came without any warning to Brown. So as they lay convalescing in their hospital beds, he asks Jones why he did not holler. Jones admits that he froze when he heard the pop of the booby trap. Jones feels badly because if he had hollered, the other men probably would not have been wounded.

> (All troops entering the Reliable Academy are given instructions to holler "HIT IT" and to hit the ground immediately upon hearing the pop of a booby trap. Yet, surveys show that when confronted with reality, inexperienced soldiers sometimes just don't react.)

And so it goes, even though A Company had two VC body count for the day, three men had been wounded, two seriously.

> (In April 1969, 41 percent of the 9th Division soldiers killed in action and 63 percent of those wounded were casualties from booby traps. Booby traps are the single most important casualty producer in the 9th Division area.)

This, then, is the story of a booby trap casualty. The patterns, types, locations and enemy reactions are all predictable. To prevent such incidents, the 9th Division collects the most detailed statistics, disseminates vital tactical information, teaches refresher courses, follows up with reaction tests, and constantly exhorts troops to utilize proper combat formations and distances between soldiers. Notwithstanding, in the last analysis it is the action of the individual soldier that will detect enemy booby traps and insure his and his buddies' safety.

REMEMBER!

Be Alert
Utilize the expertise of the Tiger Scouts
Don't walk on trails and rice paddy dikes if you can help it
Probe jungle foliage carefully
Watch where you step
Change point men often when you are tired
Don't bunch up
And when the above don't work and you hear a booby trap "pop," holler "HIT IT" and hit the ground

You, the rice paddy soldier, are the most important asset the 9th Division has. Don't be a booby trap casualty.

Hunt, C/S

Appendix D
Prisoner Phan Xuan Quy: Biographical Information and Thanh Phu Battle Account

Biographical Information

    Phan Xuan Quy—Headquarters Secretary, 261 B Battalion

On 11 April 1969, approximately 12 kilometers southwest of My Phuoc Tay, elements of the 7th ARVN Division discovered a VC hospital and captured a PW identified in subsequent interrogation as Phan Xuan Quy, Headquarters Secretary of the 261 B Battalion. This position is roughly equivalent to that of Battalion Adjutant. The subject is an intelligent, well educated and hardcore Viet Cong. He had been wounded on five occasions in contact with ARVN elements and did not desire to rally to GVN.

    Phan Xuan Quy was born in the 1st District of Saigon in 1949. He lived with his stepfather as his mother had been imprisoned during the reign of Bao Dai for reasons unknown to Quy. Quy's mother was released from prison in 1954 and died a few days after her release. According to Quy, her last words to him was a request that he avenge her death and the wrongs she had suffered at the hands of the Bao Dai regime. His disaffection and dissatisfaction with the GVN and the later rallying to Viet Cong ranks can be traced to this. In 1958 Quy's stepfather died and Quy went to live with Pham Binh, a friend of his father. From 1958 to 1963 Quy attended school in Saigon. In 1963, Quy moved to the capitol of Cambodia, where he attended a private school until 1966. While in this school Quy became fluent in both the French and the Cambodian languages. In January of 1966 Quy went to work for the Doc Lap newspaper, a neutralist newspaper in the capitol of Cambodia. In February he joined the Viet Cong to as he stated "Fight for the country he loved so much." He attended basic training and NCO school in Back Lien (P), Cambodia, for five months. In July of 1967 he was assigned to the VC 502 Battalion as a squad leader. In August of 1968 he was transferred to the 261 B Battalion, where he was promoted to the rank of platoon leader. In March of 1969 he was made Battalion Headquarters Secretary. On 11 and 12 March his battalion was decimated by elements of the 9th Infantry Division at Thanh Phu (V), Cai Be (D), Dinh Tuong (P), Republic of Vietnam. On 11 April 1969 he was captured by elements of the 7th ARVN Division while he was a patient in a VC hospital where he was recovering from wounds incurred from a booby trap on 10 April. He was subsequently turned over for interrogation to the 9th Infantry Division and has voluntarily provided the information concerning a contact between his unit, the 261 B Battalion, and elements of the 9th Infantry Division.[1]

Interrogator's Comments:

It is believed that the subject, as Battalion Secretary, wrote an account of the battle for the Battalion Commander, which was to be sent to the Headquarters Dong Thap I Regiment of MR II for possible preparation of a unit citation. He admitted discussing the battle with all the unit officers.

    INTERROGATOR: SP5 ROBERT T. KOT,
        9TH MI Detachment
    INTERROGATOR: SSG HUYNH VAN MAI,
        9TH MI Detachment

An Account of
The Battle of Thanh Phu
by
Prisoner Phan Xuan Quy

The 261 B Battalion with four companies and a headquarters section totaling 268 men arrived to Thanh Phu (V) at 0200 hours on the morning of 11 March 1969 after many hours of traveling from Hau My (V). The time for travel varies depending upon the situation and whether or not bunkers are available at the new site. This day we started at 1700 hours. On arrival the battalion was joined by 30 guerillas of Thanh Phu (V) and though very tired and hungry, immediately started building bunkers (usually 10 meters apart), and camouflaged the area because of constant fear of air and artillery strikes.

At 0630 hours, 11 March 1969 we suddenly received word from higher ranks that this morning there would be a sweep operation in our area. This message was received on a PRC-10 radio to the battalion commander by coded radio transmission from 122-X signal element. The 122-X signal company is assigned to Dong Thap I Regiment of MR II and has an element with each battalion.

Immediately we received an order from battalion headquarters to get in the bunkers and wait to see what happens in the next few hours. Our unit was tired and when we got word it was too late to move to another area with bunkers. We did not want to move during the daylight. Besides it usually takes us one to two hours to prepare to move because we have to raise our sunken sampans hidden in the small canals used to move our heavy weapons.

Two hours passed, then three hours, so I felt nothing was going to happen. I went out to look for some fish in the nearby canal, since I had not eaten since the day before. We get 28 piasters a day with which to buy rice. We spend very little in the first part of the month, saving seven or eight piasters a day with which to buy a duck or chicken for the squad or platoon to have an interesting party. A party for the morale of the unit and decorations are given at this time.

About a half an hour later (1030 hours, 11 March 1969), a small helicopter came into the area (C3) and flew around several times. We call this the "Staff Officer's" helicopter and when it visually recons the area, we know from past experience that US troops would definitely have an operation in that area. We had standing orders not to fire on helicopters when hiding in an area.

Suddenly another two helicopters came in and flew around our area. The order was immediately given by the C3 commander to prepare for combat. I think that then one of the helicopters discovered my position. It hovered right above me. Quickly I jumped in the ditch, trying to hide. The second helicopter was coming over fast and it looked like it was going to open fire on me. I jumped from the ditch and crawled to my bunker. As the helicopter came around again, I saw the ditch where I had been receive rockets and gunfire. The helicopters were dropping the "crying gas" and a marsh grass fire was set off by smoke grenades. To defend against the gas, we placed a wet cloth across the bunker openings, then lit a candle or burner to cause any gas which might penetrate the bunker to rise to the ceiling while we remained on the floor. This was 100 percent effective. The other method we use is to urinate on a towel and place it over the face. After the attack, we use a "Chinese Oil" to clear the "crying gas" from our skin.

At 1130 hours, 11 March 1969, I could see in the distance some helicopters coming from the south. Immediately I stood up on the top of the bunker where I could observe them. I could see five helicopters landing troops over 300 meters from my position [see map 3]. The US helicopter assaults were very fast and well done, allowing us no time to move out. US troops came in almost immediately after the first two helicopters dropped the smoke grenades.

They were all Americans without a doubt, because they were tall and had huge bodies. They started to move in our direction. C3 element got ready to hold their position and had their gun emplacements ready for them. Then I could see them advancing through the booby trap area which the Thanh Phu (V) Guerrillas had set up for our unit as a defense. Local guerrillas are used to lay booby traps to protect the flanks of the battalion. They had set up these booby traps in three rows around our defense, each row with five meters between booby traps and ten meters in depth between each row.

We had given the Thanh Phu (V) Guerrillas 150 grenades to set up for us plus they had some of their own. The Guerrillas' position was set up along the south bank of Nguyen Van Tiep Canal four kilometers from the ARVN Special Forces of My Phuoc Tay Camp to the east. This area was familiar with the local guerrillas and main ways the ARVN Special Forces would come in. The guerrillas were spread out in this area which already had old bunkers there.

(1200 hours, 11 March 1969) US troops were moving fast, so I knew they did not have any idea the booby traps were there. Suddenly I heard some booby traps explode. Five US soldiers in the front element went down and were wounded or dead. Then the entire US element stopped, lay down for five minutes and started advancing again. I think US troops were staying too close together during movement. US troops moving single file, too close together causing many booby trap casualties.

I could feel the intensity of the heat on my face from the grass burning and the soldiers around me were coughing from the black smoke. Then I

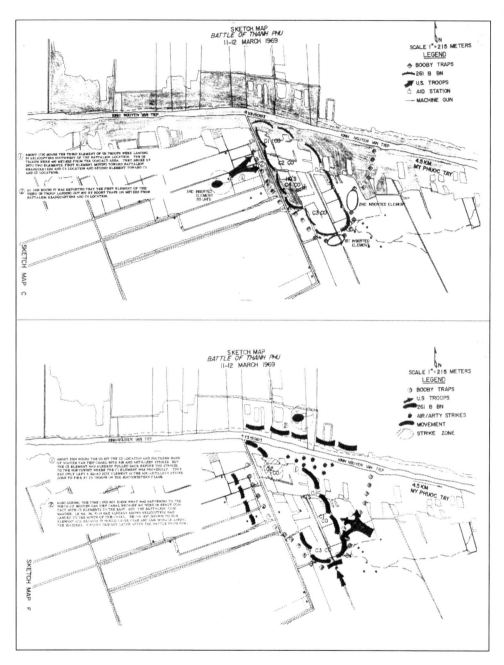

Map 3. Sketch maps, Battle of Thanh Phu, 11–12 March 1969

was informed that two killed in action and two wounded in action had resulted from the time the very first two helicopters had flown over our location (C3). US troops were still advancing, but now were dividing into two single file elements. They were 40 meters away from our location . . . 20 meters . . . ten meters. I remember seeing the tactic of advancing and dividing into single file elements being used by the ARVN's.

I heard someone yell "Fire!" To the right of my position two submachine guns swiftly spit out ammo at US troops. Meantime I gave the order to the machine gunner in my area to fire on the second part of the US element. I was put in charge of the machine gun in that area by the C3 commander, Ba Kiet, 37, K-54, when the positions were first set up. I had been ordered from battalion headquarters to stay with C3 element as acting platoon leader.

We had them pinned down at this point. Then I saw two helicopters fly over our C3 location and opened up, killing two soldiers and wounding three more to the west of my location. In my opinion US troops were moving in large groups allowing us to easily pin down the element with one or two machine guns. They waited until they were too close to our position to deploy any assault tactics. US troops believe that because they cannot see the VC in the area, the VC are not there.

About 1300 hours the reinforced elements of the US were landing 15 more helicopters to the east of C3 location approximately 350 meters away [see map 3]. During this time the US was dispersing in that area where the second insertion took place. Two 82mm mortars from C4 (Heavy Weapon) element were firing away. I heard many mortar rounds hit that US element, but they were still advancing. The C4 Heavy Weapon element was set up in the middle of the defense area to protect battalion headquarters and provide artillery support to the infantry companies.

The US second inserted troop landing had started to break up into three elements to try to penetrate the battalion defense position: first element concentrating on C4 location; second element moved north to Thanh Phu Guerrillas position guarding the aid station in that area; third element was heading southwest to C3 location where I was. I ordered the machine gunner at my position to turn and fire at the second inserted landing of US troops to the east. At this time C3 and C4 machine gun elements were concentrating to fire on US advancing elements and it was effective because we had "dug in" positions and bunkers. Then the C3 commander, Ba

Kiet, near my position, gave the order to concentrate B40's and antitank weapons on the dikes and small canals which US soldiers were using as protection when advancing to the company defense positions from the east. Also he gave the order to start evacuating the wounded. The wounded are carried to a battalion aid station for emergency treatment by members of the battalion. From that point they were transported by recruited civilians to a hospital supporting the unit. Nylon hammocks are often used to transport the wounded.

About 1600–1700 hours, the C3 location was hit by helicopters. This time they destroyed two submachine guns and killed two west of my location. Suddenly there was a terrific flash to the north of C3 location near the Nguyen Van Tiep Canal where the Thanh Phu Guerrillas were located. No more firing was coming from that area. Later after the battle, I found out that this air strike knocked out the guerrilla position resulting in 30 Thanh Phu Guerrillas killed. At 1700 hours there was one helicopter flying at low altitude at C3 location and spotted our position, forcing us to open up with AK-47 and machine gun fire. The helicopter was hit and started shaking as it flew back toward Highway 4 in a southwest direction.

The recon reported the following to battalion headquarters and this information was passed to the companies by field phone:

> About 1730 hours the third element of US troops were landing 20 helicopters southwest of the battalion location [see map 3]. The US troops were 400 meters from the contact area. They broke up into two elements; first element moving toward battalion headquarters and C4 location and second element toward C1 and C2 locations. At 1800 hours it was reported that the first element of this third US troop landing got hit by booby traps 150 meters from battalion headquarters and C4 location. At 1830 hours it was reported that this third reinforced element then had pulled back 100 meters and deployed as a blocking force along the southwestern flank of our battalion location.

I saw US troops using sniper fire tactics and launching M-79 rounds at our elements during this time. The battle area was covered with thick black smoke from the marsh grass fire. About 1830 hours US troops to the east (second US troop landing) started to strongly assault the C4 Heavy Weapon element located in the center of the battalion defense formation. Two helicopters and two jets had already destroyed the C4 Heavy Weapon position that had been blocking US troops coming from the east earlier. Many VC were lying around dead or wounded in that area. This caused the C1 (100 men) to reinforce the C4 element which was hit so badly and to continue to prevent US troops from penetrating that area by acting as a screening force. C2 had only 40 men and did not reinforce C4. C3 element was still holding off US elements to the south with small arms fire. During this time the elements kept close communication by using runners from platoon to company headquarters and field phones were used from company headquarters to battalion headquarters. (This is how C1 knew to reinforce C4.) We had a PRC-10 radio at battalion headquarters but did not use it during contact because the helicopters might discover our positions.

About 1900 hours the C3 commander, Ba Kiet, 37, K-54 ordered some of his men to look around for dead bodies and hide them in bunkers and cover others with camouflage nylon because it would be dark soon.

About 2000 hours the US hit the C2 location and southern bank of Nguyen Van Tiep Canal with air and artillery strikes, but the C2 element had already pulled back before the strikes to the northwest where the C1 element was previously. They had only left a squad-size element in the air/artillery strike zone to fire at US troops on the southwestern flank. The C2 soldiers had informed this to me after the battle. Also during this time I did not know what was happening to the north of Nguyen Van Tiep Canal because we were in heavy contact with US elements to the east but the battalion commander, Le Ha, 44, K-54 had already known helicopters had landed to the north of this canal. He did not inform to our element (C3) because it would cause fear and low morale among the soldiers. I found this out later after the battle from him.

About 2100 hours it was completely dark except for flares and the speed of the fire fight was diminishing, but sound of helicopters were heard and seen still flying around our area of defense. At this time our element (C3) was informed by the battalion commander, Le Ha, that 44 helicopters with US troops had landed and already set up all along the northern part of Nguyen Van Tiep Canal. At this time I just knew that US troops had completely surrounded our position.

About 2200 hours the recon had reported to the battalion commander, Le Ha, that the withdrawal route was found. He informed to the companies that at 2300 hours the units would start withdrawing, element by element. At 2330 hours a recon member from battalion headquarters came down to C3 position to give the word that we were to move north to Nguyen Van Tiep Canal. The strength of our element (C3) was very low at this time. Many small arms (AK-47) were lying around the bunkers where our soldiers lay dead. We placed some more of the dead in the bunkers and covered some with nylon stuff because US troops fail to check all possible places for bodies. Usually one day later a recon element goes back to check if US troops have left the area. Then they report back to battalion headquarters. A platoon size element is sent back into the area in the next few days to find the hidden bodies to bury them and to look for weapons that US troops failed to discover after the battle.

The C3 commander, Ba Kiet, told the soldiers to carry as many rifles and equipment with them as they could. I carried out a machine gun stand and an AK-47 rifle. The recon element then guided our element north to the Nguyen Van Tiep Canal. I saw, when we were withdrawing, that each soldier carried two to three small arms (AK-47, SKS, etc.). There were some flares in the sky around our defense area. In this case, where the tactical situation required rapid withdrawal, some weapons were hidden in the area of contact for pickup several days later.

About 0030 hours, when we reached the Nguyen Van Tiep Canal, the C3 element lost contact with the recon. The political officer, Bay Quyen, 27, K-54 took charge and guided the C3 on the withdrawal route. The rest of the battalion was ahead of C3 already moving west along the canal with elements ten meters apart. The battalion's main recon element was in front avoiding contact with US troops as much as possible. I would like to include here that the recon elements conducted continuous and extensive recon during the course of the contact to attempt to locate a gap in the US defense formation. They reported constantly to the battalion commander.

About 0045 hours, when the C3 element was along the Nguyen Van Tiep Canal, we began receiving M-16 and M-79 fire from the US troops on the northern bank of the canal. One round hit the machine gun stand I was carrying and I fell in a ditch. I picked up the stand and continued on. The tracers continued to fly all around us. Later the political officer found a new way to bypass traveling near the canal where the tracers were hitting. Continuous air strikes were dropping all along the canal and surrounding area. When they came close to our position, we would lie down. While *moving along the withdrawal route, we tried to run quickly to wherever the air/artillery strikes already hit. This is how we got through them. Move back when the first bombs fall. Then after the strikes, move back into the same area, as we believe the US does not bomb in the same area right away.*

Approximately 0100 hours we finally reached the area where the battalion recon element was standing guard. They showed us the 50 meter gap where the rest of the battalion had made it through. The tactics we used here were the recon element secured each side of the gap. The companies infiltrated through the gap in small groups in single file. A small force is left behind in the contact area to cover the withdrawal of the main body.

As we passed through the gap, we could hear the Americans talking loudly on both sides of us. We quietly took our clothes off upon reaching the Cha La Canal and made floating rafts out of nylon. These floating rafts hold the weapons while in the water as we swam to the other side. We did not use sampans because they can easily be detected by US helicopters. I just got out of there in time and was glad to be alive!

The air/artillery strikes could be heard in the distance as we were moving away from the contact area (0130–0200 hours). After moving out of that area for one and a half kilometers, I estimated 95 men left. The air/artillery strikes continued all night in the area of Thanh Phu.

On 13 March 1969, when we reassembled at the Trai Lon Canal after the battle, I found we had 20 deserters, leaving only 75 men left.

We discussed the battle. Before the battle we had 268 men in our unit plus there were 30 guerrillas. In the reassembly area after the battle there were 95 in the unit but 20 deserted. The 30 Thanh Phu (V) Guerrillas were killed by air/artillery strikes and general casualties were 173 men of our unit. It was unknown how many were killed and wounded of each company because the report was not made out that was to go to MR II. Since my position is secretary of the battalion at this time I have to collect the information and write a report to the battalion commander but the only thing I received was the weapon loss report. This consisted of the following:

C1 — 1 Machine gun
C2 — 1 Machine gun 1 B40 1 B40 1 60 mm mortar
C3 — 2 Submachine guns
C4 — 1 82 mm mortar 1 B40 1 Machine gun

Small arms lost in the battle were not reported. The reason I have to take a long time to make a report is because the exact personnel loss was not reported by each company commander yet.

On the day of 13 March 1969 my battalion commander reported on the radio to the 1st Regiment that: There were 1500 US troops that participated in the battle from Saigon. We were courageous and killed 150 US troops, shot down one jet aircraft and two helicopters. After this the battalion commander gave the speech in front of the soldiers that the regiment highly recommended praise to each soldier.

On 15 March 1969 at 0300 hours in the morning 20 men (subject included) of the unit arrived back at the battle area. We just arrived in the battle area and observed around the area. The truth of the area was exposed under my eyes. Oh, I could not believe any view more lonely and terrible than this. All of the trees were burned down all around the area and I could not see any grass left on the ground. Our bunkers were destroyed and out on the ground I saw dried blood all around, still smelling the odor of the dead bodies in the air. It made me feel terrible. Also the big holes that were made by bombs made me thankful I had made it out alive. We encouraged ourselves to look for the dead and bring them to the sampans forgetting the smell of their bodies. At about 1000 hours in the morning we saw the ARVN Special Forces in that area but we ran away and hid from them along the Cha La Canal, one kilometer to the west of the battle area. We had only recovered five bodies before we were forced to move. Then we returned to the units with a sentimental feeling for all our dead comrades that were lost in the battle.

EPILOGUE: *After we had returned to Trai Lon Canal the unit broke up into small groups. The regiment had already sent us three new 60 mm mortar tubes a few days after the battle. We were very tired and our morale was very low, but the battalion commander gave the word that our unit (75 men) would return to Kien Phong (P) to get reinforcements and recruit new men to fight again. On the way I got hit by a booby trap so I had to stay back at X-12 Hospital of MR II in Hau My (V). I just stayed there one night and the next morning the 7th ARVN Division soldiers swept the area and captured me and six other VC, when discovering and destroying the hospital.*

Appendix E
Reflection of a Prisoner

Prisoner Phan Xuan Quy, the former secretary of the 261 B Battalion, wrote the following reflections at midnight on 30 April 1969 while in the 9th Infantry Division POW compound.

Night is falling deeper and deeper, the breeze is colder and colder, the wind is blowing into my prison camp. Perhaps today is the 19th day of my life staying in the prison. At this time it is 12 o'clock midnight. There are two soldiers standing guard at the door of my prison camp. They wear the letters "M.P." on their sleeves. I feel they are well trained to stand guard awake. Outside at this time some jeeps pass by in a hurry out on the road, plus the roar of artillery is heard out going from this Binh Duc Base Camp (Dong Tam). The dew drops are falling thicker and thicker, the wind is blowing harder. All of this gives me a feeling of indifference. I could not fall asleep. I sat up to light my cigarette and think deeply of my life about "what could happen to me in the future." I was feeling that my future is very dark. While being a soldier, I had been wounded 5 times and about 10 times escaped out of death. I don't have any grief, but this time I worry about it. I am a young man, but somehow I always find myself in trouble. As I look back and remember the day I was captured and turned into the prison camp of the Americans. Before I got in here I always thought that I would be kept in a completely dark jail in which I could not see any rays of sunlight fall into my prison and lie in handcuffs. But, everything is the opposite. This prison camp is a large area. It contains 6 barracks, all of which are covered by canvas, and very clean area. I receive three meals a day. Some bystanders passing on the road outside just think that is a workers' sleeping barracks. The few days that have passed, I have been given good treatment. They have given me cigarettes and anything I need. Each time they brought me in for interrogation, it was a narration of mine for them, no more and no less. I simply sat down, talking friendly. Before I got here, my thinking was about the pressure and misery I would have to endure at a prison camp. Now my bad impression is replaced by the highest opinions of Americans.

Note: This reflection is taken from Maj. Clyde A. Turner III, Letter: Reflection of a Prisoner of War 1 May 1969. 9th Military Intelligence Detachment, Republic of Vietnam.

Notes

Introduction

1. Maj. Gen. Harris W. Hollis to Commanding General II Field Force, Vietnam, APO 96266, Subject: Recommendation for Award of the Presidential Unit Citation, May 1969, Headquarters 9th Infantry Division, Republic of Vietnam. Unless otherwise noted, all papers, correspondences, and other documents from the 9th Division are in the author's possession.

2. These improvements are discussed in detail in Julian J. Ewell and Ira A. Hunt Jr., *Sharpening the Combat Edge: The Use of Analysis to Reinforce Military Judgment,* Vietnam Studies (1975; repr., Washington, D.C.: Department of the Army, 1995).

1. Securing the Mekong Delta

1. Dong Tam Base COs, Briefing, 1 Dec 1967, Dong Tam Base History, Progress and Plans. Dong Tam, Republic of Vietnam.

2. William B. Fulton, *Riverine Operations, 1966–1969,* Vietnam Studies series (Washington, D.C.: Department of the Army, 1972).

2. The General Offensive and General Uprising

1. Operational Report, 9th Infantry Division, for Period Ending 30 April 1968, RCS CSFOR-65(R1), 12 May 1969, 9th Infantry Division, Republic of Vietnam.

2. Dinh Tho Tran, *Pacification,* Indochina Monographs series (Washington, D.C.: U.S. Army Center of Military History, 1977).

3. Memorandum for COMUSMACV. Incident at Pham The Hien Port on 9 May 1968, Battle of Saigon, 9 August 1968. Headquarters, 9th Infantry Division, Republic of Vietnam

4. Lt. Col. L. A. Spirito, Subject: Identification of VC Base Areas, 12 August 1968. Headquarters 9th Infantry Division, Republic of Vietnam.

5. J-2, Joint General Staff, Republic of Vietnam Armed Forces, "Communists' Assessment of the RVNAF," Saigon, 1973.

3. Enhancing Combat Capabilities

1. A. W. McFadden, Surgeon's Information Letter 34-69: Management of Skin Diseases by Battalion Surgeons in the Tropics. 9th Infantry Division, Republic of Vietnam, 1969.

2. Benjamin G. Withers, *Skin Disease in the U.S. 9th Infantry Division, Republic of Vietnam* (Washington, D.C.: Headquarters U.S. Army Material Command, 1996); Patrick W. Kelley, *Military Preventive Medicine, Mobilization, and Deployment*, vol. 1 (Washington, D.C.: Borden Institute, Walter Reed Army Medical Center, 2003).

3. Edwin A. Deagle Jr., "Tactical Operations in the Delta," Headquarters, 9th Infantry Division, Republic of Vietnam, 1968; John O. B. Sewell, "Tactical Concepts in Delta Warfare," 9th Infantry Division, Republic of Vietnam, 1968.

4. Edwin A. Deagle Jr., "Staff Study: Utilization of Non-Organic Aviation Assets," Headquarters, 9th Infantry Division, Republic of Vietnam, 1968.

5. DA Form 1352, "Summary of Major Units Reporting Aircraft," February 1969, Army Division, USARV Aviation Data Analysis Center, Republic of Vietnam.

6. Commanding General, 9th Infantry Division, to Commanding General, II Field Force Vietnam, regarding Utilization of Army Aviation Assets, 9th Infantry Division, Republic of Vietnam, 7 May 1969.

7. Letter, Headquarters 9th Infantry Division, Airmobile Operations, 12 October 1968.

8. Lt. Col. Leonard A. Spirito, "Reliability of Intelligence, Resources," Headquarters, 9th Infantry Division, Republic of Vietnam, May 1969.

9. Headquarters, 9th Infantry Division, "Utilization of the Airborne Personnel Detector," Republic of Vietnam, 30 May 1968.

10. Headquarters, 9th Infantry Division, Document, Night Surveillance Aids, Republic of Vietnam, 1968.

11. John J. Bick, "Delta Rangers Employ Enemy's Own Tactics," Information Office, 3rd Brigade, 9th Infantry Division, Tam An, Republic of Vietnam, 1968.

12. Headquarters, 9th Infantry Division, "Sergeant Waldron and the Sniper Program," Republic of Vietnam, 1969.

13. Headquarters, 9th Infantry Division, "Monthly Mine and Booby Trap Report," Republic of Vietnam, 9 May 1969.

4. Pacification: The Endgame

1. Ira A. Hunt Jr., "War by Budget: How the Wars in Vietnam and Cambodia Were Lost, 1973–1975," unpublished manuscript, Washington, D.C.

2. Hamlet Evaluation System, MACV Document DAR R70-79, Republic of Vietnam, 1 Sept 1971.

3. 9th Infantry Division, "Bridge to Understanding, Civic Action Program," Republic of Vietnam, 1969.

4. Maj. Gen. Harris W. Hollis to CG III ARVN CORPS Tactical Zone, "Summary of 9th Infantry Division Activities to Thwart the VC Winter-Spring Offensive, 1 January 1969 to 31 May 1969," 9th Infantry Division, Republic of Vietnam, 31 May 1969.

5. 9th Infantry Division, pamphlet, "Organization of an ICAP," Republic of Vietnam, 1969.

6. Ira A. Hunt Jr., Report to Assistant Division Commander, Evaluation of ARVN and RF Units, 1st Brigade, 9th Infantry Division, Republic of Vietnam, September 1968.

7. Maj. Gen. Harris W. Hollis, Letter to Lt. Col. William B. Rosson (Operational Effectiveness), 9 May 1968, Headquarters 9th Infantry Division, Republic of Vietnam.

5. Third Phase of the VC/NVA General Offensive

1. Maj. John O. B. Sewell, "Captured Viet Cong Battle Maps, Enclosure 1 to The Dynamic of Delta Operations, 1968," 9th Infantry Division, Republic of Vietnam.

2. Headquarters, 9th Infantry Division, Statistical Summary, Enemy Strengths IV CTZ, Republic of Vietnam, 20 December 1968.

7. The Take-off

1. Maj. Gen. Harris W. Hollis, "History of the Battle of Thanh Phu, 11–12 March 1969," Headquarters, 9th Infantry Division, Republic of Vietnam, 29 May 1969.

2. Army Component of the Army-Navy Mobile Riverine Force, "Flexibility in the Mekong Delta, The Kien Hoa Province Campaign of the 2nd Brigade 9th Infantry Division, September 1968–July 1969," Republic of Vietnam.

3. Headquarters, 9th Infantry Division, "Tactical Notes," Republic of Vietnam, 29 May 1969.

8. Post–Dong Xuan Operations

1. Maj. Gen. Harris W. Hollis to CG III ARVN CORPS Tactical Zone, "Summary of 9th Infantry Division Activities to Thwart the VC Winter-Spring Offensive, 1 January 1969 to 31 May 1969," 9th Infantry Division, Republic of Vietnam, 31 May 1969.

9. Pacification Results

1. U.S. Senate, Committee of Foreign Relations staff report, "Index of Agricultural Production," Vietnam, May 1974.

2. Office of the Adjutant General, Department of the Army, General Order 59. Paragraph 5: Civic Action Honor Medal, First Class by the Republic of Vietnam, Washington, D.C. (emphasis mine).

3. J-2, Joint General Staff, Republic of Vietnam Armed Forces, "Communists' Assessment of the RVNAF," Saigon, 1973.

11. The Division Rotates Home

1. J-2, Joint General Staff, Republic of Vietnam Armed Forces, "Communists' Assessment of the RVNAF," Saigon, 1973.

2. 9th Infantry Division, "Statistics: 9th Infantry Division in Vietnam, December 1966–July 1969," Republic of Vietnam.

3. Ira A. Hunt Jr., "War by Budget: How the Wars in Vietnam and Cambodia Were Lost, 1973–1975," unpublished manuscript, Washington, D.C.

4. "Headquarters, U.S. Support Activities Group," NVA/VC OB Gains and Losses, 1967 through 1974. Nakhon Phanom, Thailand, 1975.

5. Office of the Adjutant General, Department of the Army, General Order 59. Paragraph 5: Civic Action Honor Medal, First Class by the Republic of Vietnam, Washington, D.C.

6. Hunt, "War by Budget."

7. Gen. William C. Westmoreland to General Sullivan, Chief of Staff, U.S. Army, 1 July 1991, Charleston, South Carolina.

Appendix D

1. Maj. Clyde A. Turner III, Letter, Subject: Thanh Phu Battle, 1 May 1969, 9th Military Intelligence Detachment, 9th Infantry Division, RVN.

Index

Page numbers in italics refer to tables, maps, and figures. Military units are indexed as spelled; for example, *5th Battalion* appears before *1st Brigade*.

Abrams, Gen. Creighton, 2, 135–36
Accelerated Pacification Campaign, 81, 86
ACT. *See* air cavalry troops
adjutant general unit, 148
agricultural production trends, 141
AHC. *See* assault helicopter companies
AH-1G Cobra gunships, 57
airborne infrared detectors, *51*
airborne personnel detectors (People Sniffers), *51,* 53, 57–60, 124
air cavalry troops (ACT)
    allocation, 43, 45
    daytime airmobile operations, 57
    encouraged to use People Sniffers, 124
    firepower of gunships, 38
    night operations, 48, 72–75
    utilization for maximum combat effectiveness, 38–41
air controllers, 36
aircraft
    aggressive management of, 43
    allocations, 43, 45
    availability, 41–42
    basing, 43
    combat effectiveness, 38–41
    control effectiveness, *40*
    maintenance program, 41–42, 112–13
    refueling and rearming, 43
    utilization, 42–43
    See also helicopter assets
Air Cushion Vehicle Platoon, 147
Air Force
    forward air controllers, 36
    preplanned sorties, 36–38
    "seal-and-pile-on" operations, 36
airmobile operations
    daytime, 56–61 (*see also* daytime airmobile operations)
    limitations on, 61–62
    nighttime, 71–78 (*see also* nighttime airmobile operations)
    tactics, 45–49
air strikes
    in daytime airmobile operations, 57
    striking the same area twice, 130
Akers, Col. W. A., 29
Alejandro, Jose T., 70
ambushes
    in Bushmaster tactics, 62–63
    frequency of, 65
    improved performance in, 113
    Night Ambush operations, 67, 114, 124
    performance review of squad ambushes, 106
    stay-behind technique, 65
    successful operations in, 65–66
    use of surveillance aids in, 64–65
    by the Viet Cong, 46
An Naut Tan, 12
AN-PPS-5 radar, 64
anti-intrusion devices, 64
AN-TPS-25 radar, 64, 72
Ap Binh Dong, Battle of, 120–22
Ap Dong Ninh, 101
armored troop carriers, 9, 24

Army Marksmanship Unit, 66
Army of the Republic of Vietnam (ARVN)
    increasing the operational effectiveness of, 92–94
    in Long An Province, 91
    in the pacification process, 86
Arruti, Lt. Mike, 52
artillery
    assistance in ambush operations, 66
    in daytime airmobile operations, 57
    fire support, 36
    in Night Hunter operations, 72
    relocating by helicopter, *37*
    rules of engagement, 143
    striking the same area twice, 130
assault helicopter companies (AHC)
    allocation, 43, 45
    in daytime airmobile operations, 57
    firepower of, 38
    utilization for maximum combat effectiveness, 38–41
aviation tactics, 45–49

bacterial skin diseases, 29
Ba Kiet, 169–70, 171, 172
Ba Lai River, 120–21
Barile, SP4 Phil, 121
Base Area 470, 33–34, 84–85, 131
battalions (U.S.)
    cutback in size of headquarters, 27
    number of snipers assigned to, 67
battalions (VC)
    communications in, 129
    recon element, 129
Baugher, Sgt. Robert F., 148–49
Ba Van, 18
Bay Quyen, 172
Bearcat (Camp Martin Cox), 10, 11, 22
Ben Duc, 112
Ben Luc, 96
Ben Luc bridge, 35
Bennett, 1st Lt. Craig, 2, 60
Benson, Col. George, 16
Ben Tre, 13, 14, 120, 133
Binh Duc Base Camp, 175
Binh Phuoc District, 101
Blackwell, Capt. Paul, 114–15

Bo Bo Canal, 66, 96, 109
booby traps
    casualties from, 69, 70, 71
    detection, 69–70
    frequent locations, 71
    multiple casualty-producing, 71
    Viet Cong use of, 69, 71
Bradshaw, Maj. Jack O., 2, 38
brigades (U.S.)
    cutback in size of headquarters, 27
    number of snipers assigned to, 67
    See also individual brigades
Bushmaster tactics
    ambushes and, 65
    described, 62–63
    improved performance in, 113
    success of, 78

Cai Be District, 140
Cambodia, 34–35, 95
Camp Martin Cox (Bearcat), 10, 11, 22
canals, as VC resupply routes, 66
Can Giuoc, 100–101, 101, 118
Can Tho, 13, 14
Cao Van Vien, 143–44
Capitol Military District, 14
casualties
    from booby traps, 69, 70, 71
    citizens, 143
    9th Infantry Division losses, 22, 153
    statistical results on, *155–56*
    Viet Cong losses in the General Offensive, 151, 153
C&C helicopters
    in an air cavalry troop, 57
    crash of, 101–2
    in Night Raid operations, 76
    in Night Search operations, 73
C-47 flareships, 100
Cha La Canal, 173, 174
Checkerboard tactics
    ambushes and, 65
    described, 63–64
    improved performance in, 113
    success of, 78
CH-47 helicopters, 36
Chieu Hoi (Open Arms) program, 30–32

Chieu Hoi personnel, 81
"Chinese Oil," 130
citizen casualties, 143
Civic Action Medal, 3, 144, 154
civic actions, 87, 89–90
Civic Action themes, 87
Clar, Capt. Edward, 131
claymore mines, 66
Cobra gunships
   in Night Hunter operations, 72
   in Night Raid operations, 76
   in Night Search operations, 73, 74
   See also gunships
collateral damage, 143
combat capabilities enhancement
   following Mini-Tet, 22–23
   helicopter assets optimization, 36–49, 112–13
   improving tactics and techniques, 54–78 (*see also* tactics)
   infantry solider optimization, 23–36, 112
   integration of intelligence, 49–54
   in May 1968, 112–15
combat medics, 139–40
combat operations
   assessing nighttime output, 107–8
   collateral damage, 143
   constant pressure concept and, 56, 110, 137–39
   integrating with pacification, 86–90, 98
   net effect of, 153
   number of, 2, 105–6, 134, 143
   optimization of, 26–27
   performance review of, 105–8
   statistical results of, 152–53, *155–56*
   utilization of all available assets in, 114–15
   Viet Cong advance notice of, 130
command and staff briefings, 54
communications, in VC battalions, 129
Communist forces
   American firepower advantage over, 36
   change of battle tactics in 1967, 12
   contest to control the rural population in the Delta, 80–81
   effect of the General Offenses on, 108–9
   goal of insurgents in South Vietnam, 4
   guerrilla war in the Mekong Delta, 79–80
   Mekong Delta as the primary target of, 6
   multitiered structure, 5
   objectives of, 153
   order of battle on 20 December 1968, 109–10
   use of conventional warfare methods, 80
   See also North Vietnamese Army; Viet Cong
Communist Party Central Committee, 21
"Communists' Assessment of the RVNAF," 145
Community Development, 86
contact teams, 148
cordon and search, 56
counterinsurgency operations, 3
"Crossroads," 37
"crying gas," 130, 166–67
CS gas, Viet Cong defense against, 130, 166–67

daytime airmobile operations
   assets for, 57
   flexibility of, 71–72
   insertions, 60
   "Jitterbugging," 57, 60, 61 (*see also* Jitterbug operations)
   light-observation helicopters in, 61
   overview, 56–57
   "seal and pile on," 61 (*see also* "seal-and-pile-on" operations)
   success of, 78
   use of airborne personnel detectors, 57–60
Deagle, Maj. Edwin A., Jr., 38–39
Decesare, Capt. Jesse, 102
D11 Sapper Battalion (VC), 133
dermatological diseases
   Operation Safe Step, 28–30
   problem of, 27
   See also foot diseases

Dinh Tuong Province
  action at My Hanh Trung Village, 125
  Battle of Thanh Hung, 131–32
  1st Brigade in, 11, 124
  hamlet control situation, *84*
  Hamlet Evaluation Survey, 86, 141–42, 153
  in the 9th Infantry Division's tactical area of responsibility, 32
  2nd Brigade in, 10
  Viet Cong Base Area 470, 33
  Viet Cong preparations for the Dong Xuan Offensive, 122
Distinguished Service Cross, 68
divisional base camp
  locating and constructing, 8–9
  Gen. Westmoreland names, 9
  See also Dong Tam
division headquarters
  cutback in overhead, 27
  locations of, 10, 11, 22, 25
Dong Nai Battalion, 100
Dong Nai Regiment, 18.
Dong Phu Battalion, 100, 101, 118
Dong Tam, 175
  aerial view, *26*
  aircraft maintenance at, 41–42, 112–13
  basing of aircraft at, 43
  divisional headquarters at, 11, 22, 25
  locating and constructing, 9
  2nd Brigade initially stationed at, 10
  as a target of Communist forces, 119
  Viet Cong attacks on, 123, 148
  Gen. Westmoreland names, 9
Dong Thap I Regiment (VC), 166
Dong Xuan Offensive
  abandoned by the Viet Cong, 132–35, 137, 139, 142
  attacks preceding, 122–23
  Battle of Ap Binh Dong, 120–22
  Battle of Phu My, 116–18
  Battle of Thanh Hung, 131–32
  Battle of Thanh Loi, 119
  Battle of Thanh Phu, 125–27, *128* (*see also* Thanh Phu, Battle of)
  effect of Allied interdiction efforts on, 123
  failure of, 152
  purpose of, 111, 119–20, 152
  9th Infantry Division's objective to prevent, 110
  9th Infantry Division's preparedness for, 112–15
  Viet Cong preparations for, 111–12, 118–19, 120, 122
"doughnut," 61, 126, 131
dry season, 7
Dry Weather Campaign
  assets allocated to the 9th Infantry Division, 114
  Dong Xuan Offensive and, 110, 112
  GVN pacification and, 85
  objective, 23
  success of, 134, 152
Dunn, PFC Gary E., 107
dust-off helicopters, 139

Eckhardt, Maj. Gen. George S., 8, 13
E-58 CS canisters, 60
82 mm mortars, 169
elimination ratio, 139
Emerson, Col. Henry E., 62, 100, 101, 102
Ewell, Maj. Gen. Julian J., 16, 56, 66, 92, 110, 135
exchange ratio, 105

farmers, life of, 81
F-100 fighters, 37–38
15th Engineer Combat Battalion (U.S.), 147
5th Battalion/60th Mechanized Infantry (U.S.), 17, 65
  action at Binh Phuoc, 101
  Battle of Phu My, 117
  Tet counteroffensive, 14
  third phase of the Communist General Offensive and, 101, 102
5th Nha Be Battalion (VC), 12, 18, 100
50th Regiment, 25th Division (ARVN), 91
finance unit, 148
firepower, of helicopter assets, 36–38
fire support bases (FSB), 84–85
1st Battle Group (VC), 111, 122

1st Brigade (U.S.)
    action at My Hanh Trung Village, 125
    Battle of Thanh Hung, 131–32
    Battle of Thanh Phu, 125–27 (*see also* Thanh Phu, Battle of)
    combat medics, 140
    in Dinh Tuong Province, 124
    fire support base in VC Base Area 470, 84–85
    Maj. Gen. Hunt as commander of, 102, 123–25
    intelligence briefings and, 103, 105
    joint operations with RF companies in Long An, 91
    location in late 1967, 11
    Night Search operations, 75, 131
    task organization, 159
    termination of operations, 150
    third phase of the Communist General Offensive and, 99–105, 151
    use of airborne personnel detectors in operations, 58–59
1st Independent Battalion (VC), 18
1st Long An Battalion (VC), 100, 101, 102, 118, 133
580th Battalion (VC), *138*
550th Battalion (VC), 120, 123
550th Local Force Company (VC), 120
514th A Battalion (VC), 123
502nd Battalion (VC), *100,* 165
516th Battalion (VC), 120–22, *138*
506th Battalion (VC), 12
560th Battalion (VC), 111, 120
520th Battalion (VC), 99, *100,* 101, *104*
FM radio, 129
foot diseases
    Operation Safe Step, 28–30, 112
    problem of, 24, 27, 28
    resolving the problem of, 112
footwear, 29
Fort Benning, 66
Fort Riley, 8
45th Infantry Platoon (Scout Dog), 147
46th Regiment, 25th Division (ARVN), 91
4010 Infiltration Group (NVA), 119
forward air controllers, 36

four-company rifle battalions
    daily operations, 26–27
    as the preferred structure for combat in Vietnam, 24–25
IV Corps Tactical Zone (U.S.), 10, 32
IV Corps (U.S.)
    Dry Weather Campaign, 23, 85, 110, 112, 114, 152
    Tet counteroffensive, 13
Fourth Military Region (Communist), 109–10
4th Battalion/39th Infantry (U.S.)
    Battle of Thanh Hung, 131–32
    Battle of Thanh Phu, 126–27
    Tet counteroffensive, 13
4th Battalion/47th Infantry (U.S.), 32, 68
4th Battalion/50th Regiment (ARVN), 96
Fulton, Col. William B., 10
fungal skin diseases, 29, 30

General Offensive and Uprising
    changes in Viet Cong tactics following, 55–56
    Communist battalions in, *100*
    effect on the Communist forces, 108–9
    failure to increase population control through, 84, 141, 142
    fourth phase, 111–12, 142 (*see also* Dong Xuan Offensive)
    implementation, 12
    net effect of, 21
    overview of, 150–52
    ramifications for the Viet Cong, 14–15
    second phase offensive, 15–21
    Tet Offensive, 12–14
    9th Infantry Division losses in, 22
    third phase, 99–105
    Viet Cong losses in, 151, 153
Geraci, Col. John, 72, 123
Giong Trom, 120
Glawinski, Sgt. Michael, 76
Go Cong Province
    hamlet control situation, *84*
    Hamlet Evaluation Survey, 141–42, 153
    in the 9th Infantry Division's tactical area of responsibility, 32, 33

Government of South Vietnam (GVN)
contest to control the rural population in the Delta, 80–81
force expansion following Tet, 15
guerrilla war in the Mekong Delta and, 79, 80
intelligence information and, 53
pacification program (*see* pacification)
recognition of the 9th Infantry Division, 143–44
the "rice war" and, 6, 141
Tiger Scouts, 30–32, *34*
grenades
M-79 grenades, 66
used as booby traps, 71
ground mobile operations, 61–64
ground surveillance radar, 64, 72
guerrillas
functions of, 5, 79–80
nighttime congregations, 75–76
See also Thanh Phu guerrillas
gunships
in daytime airmobile operations, 57
firepower of, 38
in Night Search operations, 131
striking the same area twice, 130
See also Cobra gunships
GVN. *See* Government of South Vietnam

Hamlet Evaluation Survey (HES)
of January 1973, 153
overview, 81–84
results of, 85, 141–42, 144
9th Infantry Division utilization of, 3
used to integrate combat and pacification operations, 86–87
Hau My guerrillas, 119
Hawk Tactics, 46–48, 103
helicopter assets
firepower, 36–38
functions, 38
light-observation helicopters, 61
medical evacuation helicopters, 139, 140
OH-6A Scout helicopters, 57
optimization of, 38–49

See also assault helicopter companies; C&C helicopters; Cobra gunships; Huey helicopters
helicopter assets optimization
aircraft allocations, 43, 45
aircraft availability, 41–42
aircraft combat effectiveness, 38–41
aircraft utilization, 42–43
aviation tactics, 45–49
helicopter gunships. *See* Cobra gunships; gunships
helicopter landing zones, no-prep policy, 45
Highway 4. *See* People's Road
Highway 5, 16
Highway QL-4. *See* People's Road
Hoi Chanhs, 139
gathering information from Vietnamese women, 90
as intelligence resources, *51*, 52, 75
statistical results on, *155–56*
See also Tiger Scouts
Hollis, Maj. Gen. Harris W., 137
Holt, Mike, 52, 125
howitzers, 36
Hudson, Capt. Joseph, 75, 76, 124
Huey helicopters
in daytime airmobile operations, 57
in Night Raid operations, 76
HUMINT, 50, *51,* 52–53, 90
Hunt, Maj. Gen. Ira A., Jr., 101–2, 123–25
Huynh Thi Kien. *See* Nguyen Thi Be
hydraulic dredges, 9

ICAPs. *See* Integrated Civic Action Programs
immersion foot syndrome, 29, 30. *See also* foot diseases
impact craters, Viet Cong use of, 129–30
infantry battalions
number in the 9th Infantry Division, 24
See also individual battalions
infantry companies
increasing paddy strength, 27–28
number in the 9th Infantry Division, 25, 26

organizational enhancements of rifle
  companies, 23–24
infantry soldier optimization
  efforts in May 1968, 112
  increasing paddy strength, 27–28
  Operation Safe Step, 28–30, 112
  organizational enhancements, 23–25
  overview, 23
  redefined tactical area of responsibility, 32–35
  relief from static missions, 25
  results of, 35–36
  Tiger Scouts, 30–32
  unit operations, 26–27
infantry soldiers
  foot diseases and, 24, 27, 28–30
  increasing strength in the field, 27–28
  optimization (see infantry soldier optimization)
infiltration
  following the General Offenses, 109
  interdiction of, 95–96
  by NVA troops, 95
  through Cambodia, 34–35
inflatable buildings, 148
infrared detectors, airborne, *51*
Infrastructure (VC), 5, 79, 137
insertions
  in daytime airborne operations, 60
  improvement of techniques in, 113
Integrated Civic Action Programs (ICAPs)
  cooperative efforts with the RF/PF, 133
  overview, 89–90
  as sources of intelligence, *51,* 65, 75, 90, 113
intelligence
  briefings, 54, 103, 105
  integration of, 49–54
  key to utilizing, 54
  significance of, 49
intelligence gathering
  integrating civic action and PSYOP efforts with, 89–90
  from Vietnamese women, 90

intelligence section, 50
intelligence sources
  Hoi Chanhs, *51,* 52, 75
  HUMINT, 50, *51,* 52–53, 90
  Integrated Civic Action Programs, *51,* 65, 75, 90, 113
  reliability, 50, *51,* 53
  sensors, 50, *51,* 53
intelligence targets, 54
interdiction
  effect on the Dong Xuan Offensive, 123
  of infiltration, 95–96

Jitterbug operations, 57
  described, 60
  improvement of techniques in, 113
  to interdict infiltration, 96
  success of, 61, 78
  See also daytime airmobile operations
judge advocate unit, 148

Kampong Som, Cambodia, 34
K-4 Battalion (NVA), 96, 118, 133, *138*
K-5 Battalion (NVA), 118, 133, *138*
K-6 Battalion (NVA), 116–18, *138*
Kidd, Sgt. Michael, 131
Kien Hoa Province
  ambush operations by 3/47th Infantry, 65–66
  Dong Xuan Offensive, 111
  hamlet control situation, *84*
  Hamlet Evaluation Survey, 85, 141–42, 153
  in the 9th Infantry Division's tactical area of responsibility, 32
  2nd Brigade in, 26, 85, 133
  Viet Cong activity in, 32–33
  Viet Cong preparations for the Dong Xuan Offensive, 122
Kien Phong Province, 33–34, 111
Kien Tuong province, 33
Kinh Doc Canal, 16
Kinh Tong Doc Luc Canal, 125

landing zones, slicks at, *59*

leaflets
    in the pacification program, 87
    Viet Cong, *88*
leaks, 130
Le Ha, 171
light-observation helicopter, 61
local force companies, 5, 75–76
Loeffke, Maj. Bernard, 87
Long An Province
    Battle of Phu My, 116–18
    Dong Xuan Offensive, 111, 122
    evaluation of ARVN and RF units in, 91
    hamlet control situation, *84*
    Hamlet Evaluation Survey, 141–42, 153
    in the 9th Infantry Division's tactical area of responsibility, 32
    operations to interdict infiltration in, 96
    3rd Brigade in, 10, 11
    Tet Offensive, 14
    third phase of the Communist General Offensive in, 99–105
Long Binh, 13
Long Khanh Province, 11
loudspeakers, 87
LTL-5A road, 35

main force units (Communist), 5
maps
    of the Battle of Thanh Phu, *168*
    of counter operations of the 520th Battalion, 101, *104*
    Viet Cong use of in after-actions reports, 19
MASH hospitals, 148
McFadden, Col. A. W., 28
McMinn, 1st Lt. Hubert, 61
mechanized battalions, 24. *See also individual mechanized battalions*
medical battalions, 147
Medical Civic Action Program (MEDCAP), 89, 90, 133
medical evacuation helicopters, 139, 140
medics, 139–40

Mekong Delta
    activation of the 9th Infantry Division in, 8–11
    agricultural production trends, 141
    apogee of Communist influence in, 151
    collateral damage in, 143
    Communist infiltration, 95
    contest to control the rural population, 80–81
    effect of Viet Cong activities in, 4, 6
    the guerrilla war in, 79–80
    GVN gains in population control in, 142
    importance of securing, 4, 6
    overview of 9th Infantry Division's operations in, 150–52
    physical characteristics, 6–8
    as the primary target of the Communist insurgency, 6
    requirement for improved security, 6–8
    Viet Cong base areas, 8, 33–35, 84–85, 131
    Gen. Westmoreland's decision to introduce forces into, 4, 8
M-14 rifles, 66
Military Region IV (U.S.), 154
Military Region 2 (VC), 46
"Mine and Booby Trap Report," 69
mines, 66, 69–71
Ministry of Revolutionary Development, 81
Mini-Tet Offensive
    changes in Viet Cong tactics following, 55–56
    Communist battalions in, *100*
    failure of, 151
    9th Infantry Division actions in, 15–21
    9th Infantry Division mechanized battalions and, 24
Mobile Riverine Force (MRF)
    concentrated on Kien Hoa province, 26
    early success of and Viet Cong response to, 11

establishment of, 10
Tet counteroffensive, 13–14
See also 2nd Brigade
Mo Cay, 37
monsoonal seasons, 7
Montro, Richard, 140
mortar attacks, 148
mortars, 169
MRF. *See* Mobile Riverine Force
M-79 grenades, 66
M-16 rifle training, 67
Muniz, PFC Rodney L., 119
Muoi Xuong, 18
My Hanh Trung Village, 125
My Phuoc Tay, 125
My Phuoc Tay Camp (ARVN Special Forces), 167
My Tho, 9, 13, 119, 123
My Tho River, 123

National Liberation Front, 26
National Police
   Battle of Saigon, 16
   intelligence information and, 53
   in support of pacification, 81, 86
Newkirk, David G., 48–49
Nguyen Thi Be, 17–19
Nguyen Van Tiep Canal, 167, 170, 171, 172
Nha Be, 13
Night Ambush operations, 67, 114, 124
Night Hunter operations, 72–73
night observation devices, 64
night operations, 48
   assessing effectiveness of, 107–8
   Bushmaster tactics, 62–63
   company-sized Checkerboard tactics, 63–64
   importance of developing, 56
   Night Ambushes, 67, 114, 124
   use of snipers in, 67
   See also nighttime airmobile operations
Night Raid operations, 75–78, 124
Night Search operations
   increased effectiveness of, 113–14
   1st Brigade and, 124, 131

   operations to interdict infiltration, 95
   overview, 73–75
   performance review, 108
   2nd Brigade in Kien Hoa, 133
   3/60th Infantry and, 73–75
nighttime airmobile operations
   1st Brigade and, 124
   need for improving, 71–72
   Night Hunter, 72–73
   Night Raid, 75–78, 124
   Night Search (*see* Night Search operations)
9th Aviation Battalion (U.S.)
   Battle of Thanh Hung, 131
   maximization of aircraft availability, 41
   Night Raid operations, 77
   Night Search operations, 74–75
9th Infantry Division (U.S.)
   Gen. Abrams on the performance of, 135–36
   activation, 8–11
   analytical approach to operations, 2
   assigned and attached units, 157–58
   attrition of Communist forces and, 97
   awards received by, 3, 143–44, 154
   casualties in, 22, 153
   constant pressure concept and, 56, 110, 137–39
   contribution of all units to the success of, 147–49
   dual focus of, 79
   enhancement of combat capabilities (*see* combat capabilities enhancement)
   GVN recognition of, 143–44
   initial tactical area of interest, 10
   mechanized battalions, 24
   mission of, 3, 79, 154
   net effect of combat operations, 153
   number of infantry battalions in, 24
   number of infantry companies in, 25
   number of operations engaged in, 2, 105–6, 134, 143
   overview of operations in the Mekong Delta, 150–52
   performance of, 2, 3

9th Infantry Division (U.S.) (*continued*)
  performance review of combat operations, 105–8
  preparedness for the Dong Xuan Offensive, 112–15
  problem of finding the enemy after Tet, 21
  1969 quarterly operational report, *135*
  rotation home, 150
  statistical results of combat operations, 152–53, *155–56*
  successes in April and May 1969, 137–38
  successes of the first quarter of 1969, 132–35
  tactical area of responsibility, 22, 25, 32–35
  task organization, 159
  Gen. Westmoreland on, 154
  See also specific units
9th Military Intelligence Unit (U.S.), 127
9th Signal Battalion (U.S.), 147
9th Supply and Transportation Battalion (U.S.), 147–48
NITECAPS, 90
North Vietnam
  assessment of the pacification program, 144–46
  goal of the insurgency in South Vietnam, 4
  recognition of the success of the 9th Infantry Division, 3
  support to the Viet Cong, 8
North Vietnamese Army (NVA)
  in the Battle of Saigon, 19
  increasing role of in war, 153
  infiltration into the Delta, 95
  use of Cambodia for supply and infiltration, 34–35
  use of conventional warfare methods, 80
  See also Communist forces
NVA. *See* North Vietnamese Army
nylon boot socks, 29

O'Connor, Maj. Gen. George G., 13, 16
offset illumination, 74

OH-6A Scout helicopters, 57
"oil blob strategy," 5
105 mm howitzers, 36
191st Assault Helicopter Company (U.S.), 125
107 mm rockets, 17, 111
126th Regional Force Company (VC), 120, 121
122-X Signal Company (Communist), 166
1097th Transportation Company (Medium Boat), 147
Open Arms (Chieu Hoi) program, 30–32
Operation Safe Step, 28–30, 112

pacification
  Accelerated Pacification Campaign, 81, 86
  Civic Action themes in, 87
  Communist objective to defeat, 111
  contest to control the rural population, 80–81
  goal of, 5
  Hamlet Evaluation Survey and, 81–84
  integrated efforts in, 3
  integrating combat operations with, 86–90, 98
  interdiction of infiltration, 95–96
  invading Viet Cong base areas, 84–85
  9th Infantry Division activation and, 8–11
  the 9th Infantry Division's mission and, 79
  North Vietnamese assessment of, 144–46
  "oil blob strategy," 5
  RVNAF commitment to and cooperation in, 80, 90–95, 113
  stages in, 85–86
  status in the mid 1960s, 5–6
  success in, 3, 5, 80, 97–98, 141–43
paddy strength, increasing, 27–28
Paris peace negotiations, 119–20
peasants, life of, 81
People Self Defense Force (PSDF), 15, 86, 151, 152

People Sniffers, *51,* 53, 57–60, 124
People's Road, 13, 35
Perkins, Capt. William, 77–78
Phan Xuan Quy
   account of the Battle of Thanh Phu, 165–74
   biographical information, 164–65
   capture of, 164, 165, 174
Phoenix Program, 81
Phu Loi II Battalion (VC), 100
Phu My, Battle of, 116–18
Phuoc Binh, 111
Phuoc Lam, 102
Phu Tho Race Track, 14
pick-up zone, *62*
pilot hours, 42–43
pilots
   bravery of, 48–49
   in Night Raid operations, 77
Plain of Reeds, 35, 66, 96, 109, 119
platoons
   ambush operations, 65
   Bushmaster tactics, 62–63
point man, 70
PRC-10 radio, 171
prisoners of war
   captured during the Battle of Phu My, 118
   captured during the Battle of Saigon, 19
   fear of being captured by Americans, 130–31
   as intelligence resources, *51,* 52–53
   interrogated from the Battle of Thanh Phu, 127–28
   lessons learned from, 128–31
   number captured in early 1969, 139
   "Reflection of a Prisoner," 175–76
   statistical results on, *155–56*
   from the 265th Battalion, 118
   See also Phan Xuan Quy
propaganda, by the Viet Cong, 87–89
propaganda leaflets
   in the pacification program, 87
   Viet Cong, *88*

psychological operations (PSYOP), 87, 89
Purdy, Maj. John, 77

Queen's Cobra (Royal Thai Army Regiment), 11

Rach Ba Tri Rom, 121, 122
Rach Cau Pheng, 121, 122
Rach Kien, 103
Rach Kien District, 91
radar
   Battle of Saigon and, 16, 65
   ground surveillance radar, 64, 72
   in Night Hunter operations, 72
   side-looking airborne radar, *51,* 53
   used in setting up ambushes, 64–65
radio, 129, 171
Rainville, Col. Rod, 133
Rangers, 76
Recommendation for Award of the Presidential Unit Citation, 2
"Recondo" troops, 132
recon elements (VC), 129
Regional and Popular Forces (RF/PF)
   in cooperative efforts during early 1969, 133
   coordinated efforts in Long An, 94–95
   expansion following Tet, 15, 151–52
   increased responsibilities of, 25
   increasing the operational effectiveness of, 92–94
   in joint operations, 91
   in support of pacification, 81, 86, 91, 92
Reliable Academy, 67
Republic of Vietnam Armed Forces (RVNAF)
   commitment to pacification, 80
   Communist assessment of, 145–46
   cooperation in pacification, 90–95, 113
   in cooperative efforts during early 1969, 133
   evaluation program for, 92
   expansion following Tet, 15
   increasing the operational effectiveness of, 92–94

Republic of Vietnam Armed Forces (RVNAF) (*continued*)
  intelligence information and, 53
  success of the pacification program and, 146
rice paddies, 7, *9*
rice paddy dikes, 7
"rice war," 6, 141
rifle battalions
  daily operations, 26–27
  organizational enhancement, 24–25, 35
rifle companies, 23–24, 35
riverine force
  artillery fire support, 36
  joint development with the Navy, 9
  See also Mobile Riverine Force
roads
  Highway 5, 16
  People's Road, 13, 35
  significance of, 35
rockets, 17, 111
Route 4. *See* People's Road
Royal Thai Army Regiment (Queen's Cobra), 11
rural population
  contest to control, 80–81
  pacification (*see* pacification)
  See also Vietnamese villagers
RVNAF. *See* Republic of Vietnam Armed Forces

Saigon
  Battle of, 16–21, *100*
  Tet Offensive, 13
  third phase of the Communist General Offensive and, 99
sampans, 7, 96, 129
Schroeder, Lt. Col. Don, 53
"seal-and-pile-on" operations
  Air Force support in, 36
  improvement of, 113
  Jitterbugging and, 61
  used by the 1st Brigade, 100, 102, 103
searchlights, 67
II Field Force Headquarters (U.S.), 13
II Field Force (U.S.), 41, 43, 150

2nd Battalion/39th Infantry (U.S.)
  Battle of Thanh Phu, 125–27
  capture of enemy prisoners, 52–53
  combat medics, 140
  Night Raid operations, 76–77, 124
  Night Search operations, 74–75
  Tet counteroffensive, 13
  third phase of the Communist General Offensive and, 101, 102, 103
2nd Battalion/47th Infantry (U.S.), 96, 147
2nd Battalion/60th Infantry (U.S.)
  attacked at An Naut Tan, 12
  Battle of Phu My, 117
  Battle of Thanh Loi, 119
  Jitterbug operations to interdict infiltration, 96
  Tet counteroffensive, 13
  third phase of the Communist General Offensive and, 101, 102, 103
2nd Battalion/47th Mechanized Infantry (U.S.), 13, 17, 94–95
2nd Brigade (U.S.)
  actions of Capt. Paul Blackwell, 114–15
  airmobile operations near Mo Cay, 37–38
  Battle of Ap Binh Dong, 120–22
  concentrated on Kien Hoa province, 26
  fires support base in Kien Hoa, 85
  initial location, 10
  as the Mobile Riverine Force, 10, 11 (*see also* Mobile Riverine Force)
  successes in March 1969, 133
  task organization, 159
  termination of operations, 150
  Tet counteroffensive, 13–14
2nd Independent Battalion (VC)
  at An Naut Tan, 12
  Battle of Saigon, 16, 18, 19
  in the General Offenses, 100, 102
2nd Long An Battalion (VC), 133
Second Military Region (Communist), 33
security, 130
seismic intrusion detectors, 65
sensors, 50, *51,* 53
709th Maintenance Battalion (U.S.), 41, 147

7th Division (ARVN)
    capture of Phan Xuan Quy, 164, 165, 174
    cooperation with the 9th Infantry Division, 90, 92
    Tet counteroffensive, 13
7th Squadron/1st Cavalry (U.S.), 107, 131
75th Infantry (Ranger), 65, 117
Sewell, Maj. John O. B., 38
side-looking airborne radar (SLAR), *51,* 53
Sihanoukville, Cambodia, 95
6th Battalion (NVA), 19, *100,* 123
6th Battalion/31st Infantry (U.S.)
    assigned to the 9th Infantry Division, 24
    Battle of Saigon, 17
    Battle of Thanh Hung, 131
    Battle of Thanh Phu, 126–27
    night snipers, 67
    third phase of the Communist General Offensive and, 100–101
65th Infantry Platoon (Combat Tracker), 147
skin diseases. *See* dermatological diseases
slicks, *59, 60*
sniper program
    development of, 66–67
    increased effectiveness of, 113
    performance review, 108
snipers
    accuracy of, 67–68
    in ambush operations, 65
    development of a sniper program, 66–67
    effectiveness of, 68, 114
    in night ambushes, 67, 114
    numbers assigned to units, 67
    as "spotters" in Night Search operations, 74
    training for ARVN divisions, 92
    training of, 67
    Sgt. Waldron, 67–68, *69*
sniper scopes, 74
socks, 29
South Vietnam
    agrarian characteristics of, 4
    goal of the Communist insurgency in, 4

South Vietnam Army. *See* Republic of Vietnam Armed Forces
Southwestern III Corps Tactical Zone (U.S.), 32
Special Region 3 (VC), 101
Spirito, Lt. Col. Leonard, 50
"Spooky" flareship, 95, 117
spotters, 74, 113, 114
squads
    ambush operations, 65, 106
    in Checkerboard tactics, 63–64
stand-downs, 56
Starlight scopes, 64, 73
static missions, termination of, 25
stay-behind technique, 65
"Story of the Booby Trap Casualty, The" (Hunt), 71, 160–63
Strategic Hamlet Program, 5
surveillance aids, used in setting up ambushes, 64–65

tactical area of responsibility (TAOR), 22, 25, 32–35
tactical notes, 134
tactics
    ambushes, 64–66
    constant pressure concept and, 56, 110, 137–39
    daytime airmobile operations, 56–61
    ground mobile operations, 61–64
    nighttime airmobile operations, 71–78
    responding to Viet Cong evasive actions, 55–56
    responses to mines and booby traps, 69–71
    snipers, 66–68
    See also individual tactics
Tan An, 13, 14, 118, 119, 148–49
Tan An bridge, 35
Tango boats, 9, 67, 113
Tan Son Nhut Air Base, 13
Tan Tru, 118
TAOR. *See* tactical area of responsibility
Taplan, David, 29
tattoos, 19
teamwork, 107

tear gas, 60
  Viet Cong defense against, 130, 166–67
Tet holiday truce, 120
Tet Offensive
  actions in, 12–14
  assessment of, 14
  changes in Viet Cong tactics following, 55–56
  failure of, 151
  goal of, 13
  GVN force expansion following, 15
  net effect of, 21
  ramifications for the Viet Cong, 14–15
  Viet Cong tactics in, 12
Thanh Hung, Battle of, 131–32
Thanh Loi, Battle of, 119
Thanh Phu, Battle of
  actions in, 125–27
  box score, *128*
  lessons learned from Phan Xuan Quy's account of, 128–31
  Phan Xuan Quy's account of, 165–74
  sketch maps, *168*
Thanh Phu guerrillas, 165, 167, 169, 170, 173
III Corps Tactical Zone (U.S.), 10
III Corps (U.S.), 13
3rd Battalion/34th Artillery (U.S.), 122
3rd Battalion/39th Infantry (U.S.)
  Battle of Saigon, 16–17
  Battle of Thanh Phu, 127
  Jitterbug operations, 58–59
  Tet counteroffensive, 13
3rd Battalion/47th Infantry (U.S.)
  ambush operations, 65–66
  Battle of Ap Binh Dong, 120–22
  bravery in, 70
3rd Battalion/60th Infantry (U.S.)
  action at Mo Cay, 37
  Battle of Ap Binh Dong, 121–22
  snipers, 67–68
3rd Battalion (VC), 99, *100*
3rd Brigade (U.S.)
  aviation asset utilization, 39
  Battle of Phu My, 116–18
  Battle of Saigon, 19
  Battle of Thanh Loi, 119

containment of the Mini-Tet Offensive, 151
discovery of enemy caches, 138
initial location, 10
location in late 1967, 11
successes in March 1969, 133
task organization, 159
termination of operations, 150
Tet counteroffensive, 14
3rd Squadron/5th Cavalry (U.S.)
  aircraft availability maximization, 41
  Battle of Ap Binh Dong, 120, 121, 122
  Battle of Phu My, 117
  light observation helicopter team, 61
  transfer to I Corps, 23–24
3rd Squadron/17th Cavalry (U.S.), 94–95, 119
Thu Thua District, 91
tides, 7–8
Tiger Scouts, 30–32, *34*, 90. *See also* Hoi Chanhs
Timothy, Brig. Gen. James S., 68
TL-24 road, 35
TL-26 road, 35
tracker dogs, 132
Trai Lon Canal, 173, 174
tripwires, 71
truces, 120
Tu Be. *See* Nguyen Thi Be
Tu Loc, 18–19
Turner, Maj. Clyde A., III, 176
25th Division (ARVN), 90, 91, 92
211th Sapper Battalion (VC), 118
252nd Battalion (VC), *100*
294th Battalion (VC), 99, *100*
273rd Battalion (VC), 111
265th Battalion (VC), 13, 100, 101, 118
261st A Battalion (VC), 131–32
261st Artillery (VC), *138*
261st Battalion (VC), 13, *100*, 101
261st B Battalion (VC)
  Battle of Thanh Phu, 127, 128, 165–74
  Phan Xuan Quy in, 164, 165
  recon element, 129
267th A Battalion (VC), 133
267th Battalion (VC), *138*
267th B Battalion (VC), 123, 133

263rd Battalion (VC), 13, 123
263rd Local Force Battalion (VC), 123

unattended ground sensors, *51,* 53
U.S. Army Laboratory, 29
U.S. Navy, joint development of the riverine force, 9
Usually Reliable Intelligence reports, *51,* 53

Vam Co Tay River, 109
Viet Cong
   advance warning of U.S. troop operations, 130
   base areas (*see* Viet Cong base areas)
   battalion communications, 129
   battalion recon elements, 129
   birthplace of NLF, 26
   changes in tactics following the General Offensive, 55–56
   Communist support to, 8
   contest to control the rural population in the Delta, 80–81
   countermeasures to U.S. airmobile assault tactics, 46–48
   defense against CS gas, 130, 166–67
   defense as a transitional phase, 55
   deterioration of morale, 134
   effect of Night Raids on, 76
   effect on activities in the Mekong Delta, 4, 6
   fear of being captured by Americans, 130–31
   General Offensive and Uprising (*see* General Offensive and Uprising)
   logistical use of sampans, 129
   Military Region 2, 46
   nighttime movements, 72
   order of withdrawal, 129
   persistent targets of, 109
   propaganda efforts by, 87–89
   response to the Mobile Riverine Force, 11
   Special Region 3, 101
   support and supplies infiltrated into the Delta, 95
   troop replacements from the NVA, 21
   truce declared during the 1969 Tet holidays, 120
   use of booby traps, 69, 71
   use of canals as resupply routes, 66
   use of impact craters for cover, 129–30
   use of maps in after-action reports, 19
   weapons captured from, *98*
   See also Communist forces
Viet Cong base areas
   American invasion of, 84–85
   Base Area 470, 33–34, 84–85, 131
   in the Mekong Delta, 8, 33–35
Viet Cong Infrastructure (VCI), 5, 79, 137
Viet Cong Military Region 2, 46
Vietnamese Cross of Gallantry, 3, 143–44
Vietnamese villagers
   assistance in setting up ambushes, 65
   contest to control, 80–81
   as intelligence resources, 50, 52
   life of, 81
Vietnamese women
   gathering intelligence from, 90
   in the People Self Defense Force, 15
Vinh Long, 13, 14

Waldron, Sgt. Adelbert, 67–68, *69*
Walker, 1st Lt. Robert, 77
Wallace, Col. Josiah, 16
Watson, Sgt. Wes, 65
Westmoreland, Gen. William C.
   decision to introduce forces into the Mekong Delta, 4, 8
   names the divisional base camp, 9
   on the 9th Infantry Division's Tet counteroffensive, 14
   personal interest in keeping the People's Road open, 35
   praise of the 9th Infantry Division, 154
wet season, 7
Williams, Maj. Gen. Robert, 45
Winter-Spring Offensive. *See* Dong Xuan Offensive
women. *See* Vietnamese women
wool socks, 29

xenon searchlights, 67
Xuan Loc, 13

Y Bridges, 16, 19

CPSIA information can be obtained at www.ICGtesting.com
Printed in the USA
267390BV00002B/3/P